Moses King

**The Poets' Tributes to Garfield**

THE

# POETS' TRIBUTES

TO

# GARFIELD

THE COLLECTION OF POEMS WRITTEN FOR THE
BOSTON DAILY GLOBE, AND MANY
SELECTIONS

With Portrait and Biography

---

CAMBRIDGE, MASS.
PUBLISHED BY MOSES KING
HARVARD SQUARE
1881

JAMES ABRAM GARFIELD,
TWENTIETH PRESIDENT OF THE UNITED STATES.

Moses King

**The Poets' Tributes to Garfield**

ISBN/EAN: 9783744679213

Printed in Europe, USA, Canada, Australia, Japan

Cover: Foto ©Thomas Meinert / pixelio.de

More available books at **www.hansebooks.com**

COPYRIGHT, 1881,
BY GLOBE NEWSPAPER COMPANY.

FRANKLIN PRESS:
STEREOTYPED AND PRINTED BY RAND, AVERY, AND CO.,
BOSTON.

# CONTENTS.

|  | PAGE |
|---|---|
| GARFIELD'S FAVORITE VERSES | 1 |
| PORTRAIT | 2 |
| CONTENTS | 5 |
| BIOGRAPHY | 7 |
| GARFIELD'S FAVORITE HYMN | 21 |
| AFTER THE BURIAL | 22 |
| THE TRIBUTES FROM THE POETS | 25 |

POEMS WRITTEN FOR THE BOSTON GLOBE:—

| | | |
|---|---|---|
| By OLIVER WENDELL HOLMES | | 28 |
| By JOAQUIN MILLER | | 31 |
| By H. BERNARD CARPENTER | | 33 |
| By JOHN BOYLE O'REILLY | | 33 |
| By CHARLES TURNER DAZEY | | 36 |
| By JULIA WARD HOWE | | 37 |
| By KATE TANNATT WOODS | | 38 |
| By LOUISA PARSONS HOPKINS | | 40 |
| By MARIE E. BLAKE | | 41 |
| By MINOT J. SAVAGE | | 42 |
| By FRANCIS A. NICHOLS | | 45 |
| By JOSEPH W. NYE | | 47 |

POEMS WRITTEN FOR OTHER PAPERS:—

| | | |
|---|---|---|
| By J. W. TURNER | *East-Boston Advocate* | 49 |
| By CALEB D. BRADLEE | *Boston Daily Advertiser* | 50 |
| By ERIC S. ROBERTSON | *New-York Herald* | 51 |

## CONTENTS.

POEMS WRITTEN FOR OTHER PAPERS:—

| | | PAGE |
|---|---|---|
| By CHARLOTTE FISKE BATES. | Boston Transcript | 51 |
| ANONYMOUS. | A London Weekly | 52 |
| By J. G. HOLLAND,. | | 52 |
| ANONYMOUS. | Frank Leslie's Illus. Newspaper | 53 |
| By L. M. S. | Boston Transcript | 54 |
| By GEORGE A. PARKHURST. | Lowell Weekly Journal | 56 |
| By D. GILBERT DEXTER | Cambridge Tribune | 56 |
| ANONYMOUS. | Boston Commonwealth | 57 |
| By HENRY C. DANE | Boston Transcript | 58 |
| By S. V. A. | Boston Home Journal | 60 |
| By ANNA FORD PIPER | Boston Transcript | 61 |
| By EMMA POMEROY EATON. | Boston Transcript | 62 |
| By D. P. | The Capital | 62 |
| By H. L. HASTINGS | Boston Journal | 65 |
| By HEZEKIAH BUTTERWORTH. | Cincinnati Gazette | 66 |
| By T. H. C. | Boston Transcript | 69 |
| ANONYMOUS | London Spectator | 69 |
| ANONYMOUS. | Andrews' American Queen | 70 |
| By EVA MCNAIR PARSONS | Louisville Courier-Journal | 70 |
| By WALT WHITMAN | J. R. Osgood & Co.'s new volume | 71 |
| ANONYMOUS | Puck | 72 |
| By JAMES FRANKLIN FITTS. | Philadelphia North-American | 73 |
| By E. S. B. | Publishers' Weekly | 74 |
| By ARTHUR N. WILLCUTT. | Boston Post | 74 |
| By JOHN READE | Montreal Gazette | 75 |
| By LILIAN WHITING | Cincinnati Commercial | 76 |
| By C. H. C. | New-York Tribune | 77 |
| By W. D. KELLY | Boston Pilot | 79 |

# THE POETS' TRIBUTES TO GARFIELD.

## BIOGRAPHY.

### FROM THE CRADLE.

A SCRAP OF GENEALOGY. — THE BIRTHPLACE. — FROM INFANCY TO BOYHOOD.

JAMES ABRAM GARFIELD, the deceased President of the United States, was born in the little town of Orange, Ohio, Nov. 19, 1831, and came from New-England stock. On the paternal side his ancestry runs back to Edward Garfield, who in 1635 was recorded as one of the proprietors of what is now the town of Watertown, Mass. His mother was a descendant of one of those Huguenots whom the famous "Edict of Nantes" drove from their beloved France to seek religious freedom in the New World. From the Garfields he inherited physical and moral strength; while from his mother he received that intellectual vigor and those fine mental qualities which have marked in many generations the descendants of Maturin Ballou. President Garfield's birthplace was a log-cabin, in a wilderness some fifteen miles from that modest home which he left in order to take up his residence at the White House. He was the youngest of four children, who were left fatherless eighteen months after his birth. The widowed mother held her homestead farm, and her children together upon it. Thomas, the oldest, and the only other boy, was a manly little fellow, and did what he could to help, while the sisters also made themselves useful in the household. At the early age of three years James began to attend school in a little log-schoolhouse, the site for which had been given by Mrs. Garfield. He was an apt scholar, and at the age of eight years was a good reader, speller, and writer. Books were his delight; and among the works with which he became thoroughly acquainted during his boyhood were "Josephus" and Goodrich's "History of the United States." With the Bible he was familiar from the first; for Mrs. Garfield, a devoted adherent of the "Campbellite" faith, was fully mindful of her children's spiritual interests, and carefully implanted in their minds the truths of the Christian religion. He remained at home until he was sixteen years old, pursued his studies with as much vigor as ever, did chores about his mother's place, worked for other people as he had opportunity, and proved himself a capable and industrious lad. He was about seventeen years old when he finally started to enter upon the seafaring life which he had long dreamed of. Arriving at Cleveland, to ship before the mast upon some of the lake craft, circumstances compelled him to abandon the plan; and he was led to become a driver on a canal tow-path. As driver, and then as boatman, he worked on the Ohio Canal several months.

## TO YOUTH AND MANHOOD.

OBTAINING AN EDUCATION. — CAREER AS A TEACHER. — THE FIRST POLITICAL SPEECH.

In March, 1849, young Garfield became a student in the Geauga Seminary, a Freewill Baptist institution at Chester. At the end of the term he worked at haying and carpentering. During his first year he paid all his expenses, and had a few dollars left. Teaching was his occupation during the interval between his first and second year at Chester; and as a teacher he proved himself a master in his school. It was one of those "district" schools, not yet things of the past, even in New England, the male pupils in which regard the teacher as a natural enemy. Garfield proved himself the physical as well as the intellectual superior of lads committed to his charge, and ruled them as well as taught them. After his course at Chester, young Garfield, in the fall of 1851, entered the Hiram Institute, where the course of instruction was considerably more advanced than any which he had yet taken. Devoting himself to his studies with the vigor which had marked his efforts thus far, teaching in the winters and keeping up his own work steadily, he found himself in June, 1854, not only ready to enter college, but to enter the junior class. He had paid his way, and had saved about three hundred and fifty dollars toward defraying his expenses at college. So he entered the junior class of Williams College, in this State, in the fall of 1854, and graduated in 1856 with the metaphysical honors of the class. He was now twenty-five; and, as the result of his constant self-denying toil of nearly twenty years, he had a collegiate education, a few threadbare clothes, a score or more of college text-books, his diploma, and a debt of four hundred and fifty dollars. He was at once elected teacher of Latin and Greek in the college at Hiram. The college was poor and in debt, but Garfield threw all his energies into the work of building it up. He soon became distinguished as a teacher, and students from far and near flocked to Hiram. In 1858, while teacher of Latin and Greek at Hiram, Garfield was married to Miss Lucretia Rudolph, his former pupil at Hiram and schoolmate at Chester Academy; and she soon proved herself a most efficient helpmeet. In 1856 young Garfield entered the arena of politics, becoming interested in the Kansas-Nebraska affairs. He ranged himself in the ranks of the Republican party, and became an earnest worker for its principles. His first political speech was made in Williamstown, in 1856, just before he left college, in behalf of Fremont, the first Republican candidate for the presidency. His first vote was cast at the presidential election that fall. In 1859 he was elected by a large majority to the Senate of Ohio from the counties of Portage and Summit, and, though yet scarcely twenty-eight, at once took high rank as a man unusually well informed on the subjects of legislation, and effective and powerful in debate. His most intimate friend in the State Senate was J. D. Cox, who afterwards became a major-general, governor of the State, and Secretary of the Interior. The two young senators roomed together, studied together, and helped each other in the work of legislation. Garfield pushed his law-studies forward, and early in the winter of 1861 was admitted to the bar of the Supreme Court.

## TO THE DEFENCE OF COUNTRY,

#### WITH VOICE AND ARM. — HISTORY OF GEN. GARFIELD'S SOLDIER LIFE.

When the secession of the Southern States took place, Garfield's course was manly and outspoken. He was serving in the State Senate when hostilities broke out; and, when the President's call for seventy-five thousand men was read in the chamber, amidst the tumultuous acclamation of the assemblage, he moved that twenty thousand troops and three million dollars should at once be voted as the quota of the State. When the time came for appointing the officers for the Ohio troops, Gov. Dennison offered him command of the Forty-second Infantry; but he modestly declined on account of his lack of military experience. But he was willing to serve in a less responsible capacity; and, resigning the presidency of Hiram College, he accepted a commission as lieutenant-colonel. A few weeks later, when the Forty-second was organized, he yielded to the universal desire of its officers, and accepted the colonelcy. The regiment took the field in Eastern Kentucky in December, 1861; and on the 20th of that month Col. Garfield was assigned to the command of the Eighteenth Brigade, and was ordered by Gen. Buell to drive Humphrey Marshall out of the Sandy valley. By a forced march he reached Marshall's position near Prestonburg at daybreak, fell upon him with impetuosity, and, after a sharp fight, forced him to burn his baggage and retreat into Virginia. Afterward he was ordered to join Buell's army, which was then on its way to re-enforce Grant at Pittsburg Landing. Thenceforward for a time the military career of Gen.

Garfield was merged in that of the Army of the Cumberland. He held no separate command; and hence the traces of his great military abilities are lost in the general operations of the army, or only now and then seen in the complimentary allusions to his services which were so often made by his superior officers. In August, 1862, Gen. Garfield's health failed, and he was sent North on sick-leave. As he was about leaving for home, he was assigned, by order of the War Department, to the command of the forces at Cumberland Gap; but he was too ill to accept the appointment. Upon his recovery he was ordered to Washington, and detailed as a member of the Fitz John Porter court-martial, which occupied forty-five days, and in which his great abilities as a lawyer and a soldier were called forth and freely recognized. When the court adjourned in January, 1863, Gen. Garfield was ordered to report to Major-Gen. Rosecrans, commanding the Army of the Cumberland, then at Murfreesborough, Tenn., who made him chief of staff. He remained with Gen. Rosecrans until after the battle of Chickamauga, which was his last event of prominence in military life. For his "gallant conduct and important services" in this battle (where he wrote every order but one, submitting each to Gen. Rosecrans, only to have them forwarded without alteration), he was made a major-general. This happened upon Sept. 19, 1863.

## AS A STATESMAN.

ELECTION TO CONGRESS. — A THRILLING INCIDENT. — THE MAN FOR THE CRISIS.

In the summer of 1862 he was elected to Congress from the nineteenth district in Ohio. At that time everybody supposed the war was going to end in a few months. Garfield was then with his command in Kentucky. He had no knowledge of any such movement in his behalf; and, when he accepted the nomination, he did so in the belief that the Rebellion would be subdued before

he would be called upon to take his seat in the House in December,
1863. He was elected by a majority of over ten thousand. After
his promotion to be major-general, Gen. Thomas offered him the
command of a corps; but President Lincoln, who had a high re-
gard for him, urged him to resign his commission, and take his
seat in Congress, and urged so strenuously that his advice pre-
vailed. On Dec. 5, 1863, therefore, Gen. Garfield, having served
in the army more than a year after his election, resigned, and took
his place in the National House. Just after Lincoln's assassina-
tion, Garfield, who happened to be in New York, attended, as one
of the speakers, a mass-meeting held in Wall Street, to consider
the fearful situation. Every one was wild with excitement and
grief; and the people, almost driven to madness, were determined
to wreak vengeance. What followed is best described in the lan-
guage of an eye-witness: —

"By this time the wave of popular indignation had swelled to
its crest. Two men lay bleeding on one of the side streets, — one
dead, the other dying; one on the pavement, the other in the gut-
ter. They had said a moment before that Lincoln 'ought to have
been shot long ago.' They were not allowed to say it again.
Soon two long pieces of scantling stood out above the heads of the
crowd, crossed at the top like the letter X, and a looped halter
pendent from the junction. A dozen men followed its slow motion
through the masses, while 'vengeance' was the cry. On the right,
suddenly the shout arose, 'The World!' 'The World!' 'The office
of the World, World!' and a movement of perhaps eight thousand
or ten thousand turning their faces in the direction of that building
began to be executed. It was a critical moment. What might
come, no one could tell, did that crowd get in front of that office.
The police and military would have availed little, or been too late.
A telegram had just been read from Washington, 'Seward is
dying.' Just then a man stepped forward with a small flag in his
hand, and beckoned to the crowd: 'Another telegram from Wash-
ington;' and then, in the awful stillness of the crisis, taking advan-
tage of the hesitation of the crowd, whose steps had been arrested
for a moment, a right arm was lifted skyward, and a voice clear
and steady, loud and distinct, spoke out, 'Fellow-citizens, clouds

and darkness are round about him. His pavilion is dark waters and thick clouds of the skies. Justice and judgment are the establishment of his throne. Mercy and truth shall go before his face. Fellow-citizens, God reigns, and the government at Washington still lives." The effect was tremendous. The crowd stood riveted to the spot in awe, gazing at the motionless orator, and thinking of God and the security of the government in that hour. As the boiling wave subsides and settles to the sea when some strong wind beats it down, so the tumult of the people sank and became still. All took it as a divine omen. It was a triumph of eloquence, inspired by the moment, such as falls to but one man's lot, and that but once in a century. The genius of Webster, Choate, Everett, or Seward, never reached it. Demosthenes never equalled it. What might have happened, had the surging and maddened mob been let loose, none can tell. The man for the crisis was on the spot, more potent than Napoleon's guns at Paris. I inquired what was his name. The answer came in a low whisper, 'It is Gen. Garfield of Ohio.'"

Such was the man whom the nation mourns. His pure and simple manhood was his chief characteristic. It showed itself in all his works, and in the last dark hours when he passed through the valley of the shadow of death.

## IN THE CHURCH.

**HIS DEVOTION TO THE CHRISTIAN RELIGION. — HIS ENTHUSIASM AS A DISCIPLE.**

For such a man, only a pure and simple religion was possible; and his faith was like his life, — plain and unostentatious. While a student at Hiram College he connected himself with the Church of the Disciples, a sect founded by Alexander Campbell, and sometimes called "Campbellites." This church has a large membership in West Virginia, Kentucky, and Southern and Eastern

Ohio. "Its principal peculiarities are its refusal to formulate its beliefs into a creed, the independence of each denomination, the hospitality and fraternal feeling of the members, and the lack of any regular ministry." The Scriptures are accepted without note or comment, and any member can address the assemblies. Garfield, who never did any thing by halves, entered heartily into the work of this communion, and soon became one of the most prominent members of the church at Hiram. This connection with the sect was never severed. "Almost every day," said the pastor of the Mentor Disciple Church, referring to a revival-meeting in which the President was once interested, "I would bring some one in who was hesitating, to let Gen. Garfield talk to him about some point on which he was in doubt; and the President always made it clear to him. One morning I brought in a political friend of the general's, and a prominent local politician, who had made a confession of religion the night before. When I told Gen. Garfield what his friend had done, he stepped quickly forward, and, putting one arm around his shoulder, he congratulated him, and then taking his hand said, with an impressiveness which I can never forget, 'This is right, Christian. Remember always that this is a battle where we struggle on to a beginning, but that it's in the endless cycles of eternity that our lives must be rounded and perfected.'"

## HIS WIFE AND CHILDREN.

**BLEST IN EVERY DOMESTIC RELATION. — PICTURE OF A MODEL HOME.**

An account like this which did not mention the noble woman whose heart, of all sad hearts in this great Republic of ours, is perhaps the saddest to-day, would indeed be incomplete. He met her first in the spring of 1849, at Chester, Ohio, where they were both pupils at an academy. She was then seventeen years old: that also was the age of her future husband. Her name was Lucretia Rudolph. Her father, Zebulon Rudolph, was a Maryland farmer from the Shenandoah Valley. Her mother, Arabella Mason, born in Hartford, Vt., was the scion of an old Connecticut family. There is a tradition in the Rudolph family, that one of Mrs. Garfield's grand-uncles was the brilliant soldier Marshal Ney. When Garfield went to Williams College, Miss Rudolph commenced teaching in the Cleveland public schools, continuing that work until he became, in 1858, the head of Hiram University; then they were married. They have continued their classical studies to their own pleasure, and to the advantage of their older children, whom Mrs. Garfield has thoroughly grounded in Latin and Greek. She has borne the general six children, of whom five are living. The first, a daughter, died in infancy; Harry Augustus, aged eighteen, and James R., aged sixteen, have entered Williams College, their father's *alma mater*. Mary, the daughter of the family, is fourteen years old. The younger children are Irwin McDowell, ten years old, and Abram, seven years old. The President said of her less than a year ago, "I have been wonderfully blest in the discretion of my wife. She is one of the coolest and best-balanced women I ever saw. She is unstampedable. There has not been one solitary instance in my public career where I suffered in the smallest degree for any remark she ever made. It would have been perfectly natural for a woman often to say something that could be misinterpreted; but without any design, and with the intelligence and coolness of her character, she has never made the slightest mistake that I ever heard of."

## TO THE PRESIDENTIAL CHAIR.

### HIS NOMINATION AND ELECTION. — THE LAST DAYS AT MENTOR. — GRANDEUR OF INDUCTION INTO OFFICE.

At the Republican National Convention in Chicago, in June, 1880, Gen. Garfield was chosen as the candidate for President on the thirty-sixth ballot, after the convention had been sitting ten days. At the national election in November last, he received two hundred and fourteen electoral votes, while Gen. Hancock had one hundred and fifty-five. The President-elect passed the time between the election and his inauguration in retirement at his home in Mentor, Ohio. Did the coming events cast their shadows before? It has been remembered of him since, how he clung with prophetic fondness to these few brief days of happiness at his own peaceful fireside in the companionship of his beloved wife. It has been remembered of him since, how he looked out upon the great untried sea before him with feelings that were not wholly hopeful. A correspondent recalls how, coming in to take his leave once after a visit during this time, he found the wife sitting in the room where only the firelight threw out its ruddy glow upon the earnest, thoughtful face which was turned toward him. He asked her, standing there, if she was not looking forward with pleasurable anticipations to her residence in the White House. She answered quickly, and with unaffected sincerity, "No: I can only hope it will not be altogether unhappy," — words which now seem those of an almost inspired prophecy.

At last the time drew near when the President-elect was to assume the precious dignity to which the voice of his countrymen had called him. The journey from Mentor to the capital was a hopeful and a joyful one, in sad contrast to that journey from the capital to Cleveland in which he was to figure in the coming months.

The 4th of March was a great day at the capital. Washington was decked out in her gayest. One hundred thousand people stood in Pennsylvania Avenue, between the Treasury and the Capitol grounds, and gave acclaim to Garfield as he passed. The buildings were splendidly decorated. There was a flag and a dozen fluttering handkerchiefs at every window. All vehicles were excluded from the avenue, and the people hemmed in the procession ten deep on each side. Garfield rode uncovered nearly the whole distance. The procession wound around the southern wing of the Capitol. Garfield and Hayes alighted at the Senate wing, and entered the chamber.

The procession started from the White House, the President being escorted by the first division; and, on the return, all fell into line. The route was around the south side of the Capitol to Pennsylvania Avenue, thence to the Treasury Department, and so on past the White House. During the time between 12 and 1.30 o'clock, Pennsylvania Avenue presented a remarkable sight, either from the Treasury Department or the Capitol. The crowd was continuous from First to Fifteenth Street; and, as the time for the procession to move approached, the crowd increased, so that there seemed hardly room for the military column to enter. The regular troops led the way, with Sherman at their head. Behind Sherman were three four-horse carriages, — Presidents Garfield and Hayes, Vice-Presidents Arthur and Wheeler, and Senators Pendleton and Bayard. In addition to the Cleveland troops, Gen. Garfield was attended by the Columbia Commandery of Knights Templars of the city, of which he was a member. When the head of the procession reached the Treasury Department, the avenue for its whole mile length was literally packed with people. There was a pause at this point, to enable the President to leave the column, and proceed to the grand stand in front of the White House, where he stood hours in witnessing the passage of the great military and civic concourse, which was over three hours in passing a given point. The route was then continued up Pennsylvania Avenue to Washington Circle, along K Street to Vermont Avenue, and past the Thomas statue, down Massachusetts Avenue to Mount Vernon Square, where the procession finally dispersed.

In the evening the ball was the grandest ever seen in Washington. Little they knew, who participated in the festivities of this memorable occasion, of the scenes which would be enacted in the city in a few months, — how the crowds would again throng the streets to witness a procession. Oh, how different! how the city would again be hung with drapery and flags, but with so opposite a meaning!

Of the time between the 4th of March and the following July, nothing need be said. Gen. Garfield's administration was never fairly opened. It was but a promise, the fulfilment of which never came.

## THE ASSASSIN'S HAND.

**THE TERRIBLE CRIME WHICH SHOCKED THE WORLD. — THE STORY OF A DAY OF SUSPENSE AND PAIN.**

Toward the last of June the President prepared to leave Washington for a two-weeks' trip in New England. Mrs. Garfield, who had gone to Long Branch on account of her delicate health, was improving rapidly. It was arranged that she and the two sons and a daughter, who were with her, should join the general and the elder boys, James and Harry, at New York on the afternoon of July 2.

Meanwhile the assassin Guiteau was dogging the President about the streets of Washington. Having decided not to kill him at the church, and being deterred at the depot on the 18th of June, according to his own confession, by the sad, weak, and frail appearance of Mrs. Garfield, triumph was his at last on the fatal 2d of July. Two pistol-shots, — the reverberation of which thrilled round the world, — and the wretch was hurried to the jail!

This happened on July 2, at 9.20 A.M., as the President was passing through the station of the Baltimore and Potomac Railroad to take the train. Two shots were fired from a heavy pistol, but only one ball hit him. He fell immediately. The physicians made an unavailing attempt to discover the ball at the depot. It was evident that nothing could be done in the presence of such a crowd; and the slight chances of saving the President's life depended upon placing him where he could have absolute quiet. A police ambulance was sent for, and it was backed up to the B-street entrance of the depot. The President was brought downstairs upon a stretcher. The doors were thrown open; and the crowd parted, while the wounded man was gently laid on mattresses on the bottom of the vehicle. The President was very pale and weak, but conscious. He opened his eyes, and silently waved his hand toward the crowd. Strong men sobbed at the pitiful sight. As the ambulance was driven up to the south entrance of the Executive Mansion, the President was lifted out. He looked up, and saw Private Secretaries Brown and Cook looking down from one of the windows. He smiled, and saluted them with his uninjured arm. He was taken to his bed of sickness. During the painful hours that followed, he called frequently for his wife, and several times made the pitiful inquiry, "Why did he shoot? I had done him no harm."

The President's condition was considered imminently dangerous, — so much so that his proper treatment was neglected. From the time when the wound was looked at by Dr. Townsend at 9.30 at the depot, until eight at night, it received no effection; for ten hours and a half the surgeons only administered hypodermic injections and stimulants, and did not endeavor to ascertain the true nature of the injury. At 8 P.M., when the natural consequences of contusion had in a great degree closed the channel of the bullet, an insufficient and unskilful examination was made, from which it was concluded that the missile had entered the body about two inches to the right of the fourth lumbar vertebra, between the tenth and eleventh ribs, had passed through the liver, and could not be traced farther, and that the use of the probe would be improper. It was assumed, not ascertained, that the wound was mortal. In the course of that afternoon Dr. Bliss, the physician in charge, thought that the evidences of internal hemorrhage were distinctly recognizable, and that collapse was imminent. At 6.45 P.M. he believed the patient was sinking rapidly. At that time the physicians considered the case hopeless.

Thenceforth for eighty days the President was cared for by some of the most skilled of American surgeons and physicians. From time to time there were signs of improvement, and then again of relapse; rays of hope and shadows of despair alternated; but at last, on the nineteenth day of September, at 10.35 P.M., the President died in Elberon Cottage, at Long Branch, N.J.

Though hope had gradually been going out, — though it had gone out entirely in the hearts of all but the most sanguine, — no one dreamed of the swift approach of the dread messenger. The day was an anniversary in the life of the suffering President. On the 19th of September, just eighteen years before, he had been made a major-general for his gallantry at the battle of Chickamauga. It has been remembered of him since, that he had said he thought he should die upon that day. Strange fatality!

The remains were taken, with the greatest honors ever shown an American, to Washington, where they lay in state in the Capitol until their removal to Cleveland, Ohio, where they were placed in their final resting-place in Lake View Cemetery. The day of burial, Monday, Sept. 26, was a day of mourning throughout the Union, and with all Americans who chanced to be in other countries.

## TO THE GRAVE.

A MOURNFUL PROCESSION ALL DAY LONG BY THE SPOT WHERE THE LATE PRESIDENT'S REMAINS WERE LYING IN STATE FOR THE LAST TIME.

ON Sunday Cleveland was full to overflowing. At the lowest estimate, there were two hundred thousand strangers in the city, and the number was constantly increasing. All down the length and breadth of the solemn streets, vast crowds surged all day long. The governors of eighteen States and Territories, and their staffs, and about forty mayors and city delegations from the United States and Canada, were in town for the purpose of taking part in the sorrowful exercises. In the morning the workmen had finished the catafalque, a structure worthy of the city and the illustrious dead. Long before daylight the people had formed a long line on the west side of the square, ready for the opening of the gate of the western arch. The line stretched away down Superior Street, men, women, and children, to the viaduct that spans the river valley, and far across that to the other side. A line of military guarded the long procession on either hand. The crowd was silent. There was no loud talk, no jostling, no laughter. Patiently, quietly, and as though the funeral were that of a near friend, the people waited. At last, about eight o'clock, the great gate was swung open, and the mournful procession passed through, across the square, and up the sloping platform to where the mortal remains of James A. Garfield lay in state for the last time. With heads uncovered and bowed, the people passed by. Tears were in every eye, and many wept aloud. It was a most affecting and impressive scene.

Then followed the funeral services: which were conducted by the Rev. Dr. Ross E. Houghton, who opened with prayer; the Rev. Dr. Isaac Errett, who spoke for forty minutes in a touching and impressive manner; and the Rev. E. S. Pomeroy, who closed the exercises at the Pavilion with a prayer and benediction. An appropriate feature of the services was the singing of the following verses, — President Garfield's favorite hymn: —

## "HO! REAPERS OF LIFE'S HARVEST."

Ho! reapers of life's harvest,
  Why stand with rusted blade
Until the night draws round ye,
  And day begins to fade?
Why stand ye idle waiting
  For reapers more to come?
The golden morn is passing:
  Why sit ye idle, dumb?

Thrust in your sharpened sickle,
  And gather in the grain:
The night is fast approaching,
  And soon will come again.
The Master calls for reapers;
  And shall he call in vain?
Shall sheaves lie there ungathered,
  And waste upon the plain?

Mount up the heights of wisdom,
  And crush each error low;
Keep back no words of knowledge
  That human hearts should know.
Be faithful to thy mission,
  In service of thy Lord,
And then a golden chaplet
  Shall be thy just reward.

## "AFTER THE BURIAL."

The last sad rites are over, the last sad words are spoken: dust has been returned to dust, and the spirit of James A. Garfield has gone to the God who gave it. The people of this nation stood with uncovered heads, with heavy hearts, and with tear-stained faces, by the open door of the tomb of the martyred President. Who can voice their sentiments, their sympathy, and their sorrow? All recognize it as one of those supreme occasions when words are inadequate, when the kings of poetry and the masters of prose lament the poverty of language which fails to portray the emotions of a great people.

The marts of trade were closed; the wheels of industry were stopped; the toiling millions rested from their labors; thousands of churches throughout the length and breadth of the land were filled by men, women, and children, all anxious to participate in the solemn ceremonies of the hour; and nearly all the buildings, both public and private, bore sad emblems of mourning, from the elaborate and costly display of the merchant prince to the tiny flag and little black-and-white streamers on the cottage of the humblest laborer. There were universal signs of mourning everywhere, and the pages of history will never show more pertinent and visible symbols of a nation's sorrow.

The story of the President's remarkable career from the cradle to the grave, the terrible tragedy and awful suffering which ended in death after weeks of horrible torture, the lessons of his life and of the event to the nation, were set forth by masters of oratory, while the soothing strains of music and the sweet consoling stanzas of the song-writers were added to help voice the emotions of the people. At first sight the eulogies here and there may have seemed a trifle extravagant in language; but we do not believe the picture was overdrawn in a single instance by any intelligent speaker. A man born in humble circumstances, who digs his education out of books and experience while fighting for his own maintenance and that of a widowed mother; who ascends the ladder of fame, round by round, in the face of fierce opposition and sharp competition, and in his prime has reached the highest office in the gift of the American people, — such a man deserved lasting credit, and no words of eulogy can picture such a life in colors too glowing to suit the people and to meet the requirements of the case. And "it was the deep damnation of his taking off" which brought the early struggles and striking successes of James A. Garfield so conspicuously before the eyes of the nation, and caused a deeper appreciation of the magnitude of his achievements. And it is for these reasons that no orator could find language to surpass the expectations of the people, or words even adequately to convey their appreciation of the record of the man.

Mr. Sumner, in his eulogy on Abraham Lincoln, truthfully remarked, "In the universe of God, there are no accidents. From the fall of a sparrow to the fall of an empire, or the sweep of a planet, all is according to divine Providence, whose laws are everlasting. It was no accident which gave to his country the patriot whom we now honor. It was no accident which snatched this patriot so suddenly and so cruelly from his sublime duties." These words may be aptly applied to the event the final chapter of which was written yesterday. The death of President Garfield was no accident. God saw fit, in his infinite wisdom, to bring the sad calamity upon this nation; and all bow to his powerful decree. So far as human vision can reach, it has called forth a spontaneous outburst of patriotism and sympathy from fifty millions of people; has lifted them up to a higher plane of thought and action; has shown that the people of these United States, North, South, East, and West, have again firmly riveted the bonds which make them one nation and one grand section of the brotherhoods of the earth. It has taught us to be more charitable, one toward the other, and to take that broad and comprehensive view of human nature which leads us to value men for what they are rather than for what they are not. What other lessons the event may teach us, time alone can show.

Now that the door of the tomb is closed, the great heart of the nation should go out in sympathy to that aged mother, that devoted wife, and the fatherless children. When death comes our grief is great; but there is always a certain degree of consolation in looking upon the lifeless remains of the departed. It is when the coffin has been lowered into the newly-made grave, or the door of the tomb is shut, and we go to our homes, that the complete realization comes painfully and forcibly to our minds and hearts. It is when we see the vacant chair at the table, or the chair by the window with the view that father loved so well; it is when the rooms of our home seem so desolate, and we cannot have the sad satisfaction of seeing even the cold clay which held the soul; it is when the photograph of the well-remembered face seems to look at us from its post of honor in the album, or from the wall or mantle, and we miss him in a thousand ways in the little domestic circle, — then it is the heart is heaviest, the cup of grief is filled to overflowing, and the future looks so hopelessly sad and dismal. And this is why the sympathy and prayers and tears of the nation should to-day follow the members of the Garfield family to Mentor; for, when they reach their old homestead, — which the son, husband, and father left a few short months ago full of life and hope and " with his blushing honors thick upon him," — then will their grief be most intense, and their anguish most poignant. That the God of the widow and the fatherless will watch over and bless them all the way along in their pathway of life; and that the stricken mother, the sorrowing wife, and the fatherless children may all meet the faithful son, the devoted husband, and the tender father in the grand reunion on the shores beyond, — is the sincere and earnest prayer of every patriotic heart.

—BOSTON GLOBE, Sept. 27, 1881.

## THE TRIBUTES FROM THE POETS.

JOURNALISM, to-day, makes another gigantic stride in its onward march to perfection and the complete realization of its huge possibilities. It has explored continents; its needs have compelled science to girdle the earth with a continuous electric belt; its power makes and unmakes men; its methods have annihilated distance and time as obstacles in the way of the rapid and faithful chronicling of events. And during all this gradual and steady development, it has been improving in tone and spirit: as it grows more powerful, it grows less arbitrary; as its facilities for recording the doings of the civilized world increase, it becomes more tolerant in the expression of opinions; and as it progresses in usefulness, it becomes more intellectual. The people have come to regard the press as the great educator, not alone in the department of news, but in all branches of science. It has invaded the pulpit, the class-room, the bench, the bar, the laboratory: wherever there is information which will benefit the masses, there will the journalist be found, skipping like the bee from flower to flower, and extracting the sweet honey of knowledge.

But it has invaded a new field, hitherto closed to the surging crowd, unexplored except by the few, religiously guarded, like the ark of the covenant, against the pollution which contact with the vulgar might create, unapproachable except by the priests. It has invaded the sacred groves where the bards wander in mute and rapt contemplation of the mysteries of nature, the beauties of the landscape, and the awful splendor of the firmament, — it has invaded the precincts of poetry. And for this intrusion it need offer no apology, for its purpose was praiseworthy; and, even if its motives might perchance be impugned, it can point to the result, — the touching tributes to the illustrious dead which a brilliant galaxy of American poets spread over our first page to-day.

If the public mind is puzzled over a great constitutional question; if a sudden crisis arises in the affairs of government; if the people are in doubt about the advisability of taking a certain step, — the press steps in and enlightens them. The recognized statesmen of the land, constitutional and international lawyers, are interviewed, or solicited to add the weight of their experience and the fruits of their study to the discussion. They are, by general consent, the authorized expounders of the law; and their interpretation is accepted, the Gordian knot is untied, the dispute peaceably adjusted, and the right principle established. Since the death of our lamented President, the English language has been taxed to its utmost to furnish a suitable medium for expressing the sorrow which had settled down over the land like a huge pall. These miles after miles of crape which hung in our busy streets, and which, standing out in hard lines upon bare walls, testified to the existence of a feeling of bereavement, — what was their significance? What meant the sable garb adopted by foreign courts who had never seen or known our dead? Why were the churches crowded with sympathetic mourners who sent up prayers to the throne of grace for a man who differed from them in religious belief and form of worship? What meant the universal regrets of the whole world, the general mourning and sadness of the people, the respectful, reverential tone in which they spoke of his life, his sufferings, and his death? Who could analyze all this? who could formulate a proper interpretation of the symbolic features of this terrible national affliction? Who but the poets?

And so we went to the poets, and asked them individually and separately to pass this great mass of undefined sentiment through the crucible of song, and explain to the people the secret of their sorrow. They have done so. The genial Dr. Holmes, Boston's poet-laureate, gives expression in sweetest measure to the nation's grief and the nation's hope; while the stalwart O'Reilly, aglow with Celtic fire, pictures in burning verse the mystic meaning of that terrible midnight knell which told the nation that its chosen President was dead. Joaquin Miller, who sees pictures in the majestic waving of the pines of the Sierras, and who reads the voice of Heaven in the thunder which shakes the peaks of the Rocky Mountains, tells the story of Garfield's life, and analyzes its symbolism. And Rev. M. J. Savage contributes, of his study in the paths of philosophy and theology, a clever poem full of deep sentiment. Rev. H. Bernard Carpenter and Harvard's latest accession to the minstrel choir also join in the general song, with lyres attuned to the sombre melody of the season. But not to men alone must the task be intrusted. The tender sympathy which has gone out toward Mrs. Garfield, in her great affliction, from monarch and peasant, from ruler and subject, from the great mass of humanity, has a deep significance which only woman can interpret. Those who will read the touching lines which rapidly flowed from the pens of Mrs. Julia Ward Howe, Mrs. Marie E. Blake, Mrs. Louise Parsons Hopkins, and Mrs. Kate Tannatt Woods, will feel grateful that in the broad republic of letters women's rights are not an issue, but an institution.

We have said that "The Globe" has inaugurated a new departure in journalism. We think it will prove beneficial to the public and to the poets. The thin partition of sentiment which has divided them has been torn down, and in the future their relations will be of a more intimate and cordial nature. When any great emergency arises in the future, the poets will be called on to give shape to the feelings of the people; to embody in immortal verse the sympathies, the regrets, or the indignation, of the community. And they will respond: there is a precedent for both.

With this explanation we present to our readers the Garfield Memorial "Globe," which in future years, when the onward march of journalism shall have carried it far beyond the point reached to-day, will remind another generation of what its predecessors thought out and executed.

— Boston Globe, Sept. 27, 1881.

# POEMS WRITTEN FOR THE BOSTON GLOBE.

## AFTER THE BURIAL.

### BY OLIVER WENDELL HOLMES.

#### I.

FALLEN with autumn's falling leaf,
    Ere yet his summer's noon was past,
Our friend, our guide, our trusted chief, —
    What words can match a woe so vast?

And whose the chartered claim to speak
    The sacred grief where all have part,
When sorrow saddens every cheek,
    And broods in every aching heart?

Yet Nature prompts the burning phrase
    That thrills the hushed and shrouded hall,
The loud lament, the sorrowing praise,
    The silent tear that love lets fall.

In loftiest verse, in lowliest rhyme,
    Shall strive unblamed the minstrel choir, —
The singers of the new-born time,
    And trembling age with out-worn lyre.

No room for pride, no place for blame —
    We fling our blossoms on the grave,
Pale, scentless, faded, — all we claim,
    This only, — what we had we gave.

Ah, could the grief of all who mourn
    Blend in one voice its bitter cry,
The wail to heaven's high arches borne
    Would echo through the caverned sky.

II.

O happiest land whose peaceful choice
    Fills with a breath its empty throne!
God, speaking through thy people's voice,
    Has made that voice for once his own.

No angry passion shakes the State
    Whose weary servant seeks for rest, —
And who could fear that scowling hate
    Would strike at that unguarded breast?

He stands; unconscious of his doom,
    In manly strength, erect, serene, —
Around him summer spreads her bloom:
    He falls, — what horror clothes the scene!

How swift the sudden flash of woe
    Where all was bright as childhood's dream!
As if from heaven's ethereal bow
    Had leaped the lightning's arrowy gleam.

Blot the foul deed from history's page, —
    Let not the all-betraying sun
Blush for the day that stains an age
    When murder's blackest wreath was won.

III.

Pale on his couch the sufferer lies,
    The weary battle-ground of pain;
Love tends his pillow, science tries
    Her every art, alas! in vain.

The strife endures how long! how long!
   Life, death, seem balanced in the scale;
While round his bed a viewless throng
   Awaits each morrow's changing tale.

In realms the desert ocean parts,
   What myriads watch with tear-filled eyes,
His pulse-beats echoing in their hearts,
   His breathings counted with their sighs!

Slowly the stores of life are spent,
   Yet hope still battles with despair, —
Will Heaven not yield when knees are bent?
   Answer, O Thou that hearest prayer!

But silent is the brazen sky, —
   On sweeps the meteor's threatening train, —
Unswerving Nature's mute reply,
   Bound in her adamantine chain.

Not ours the verdict to decide
   Whom death shall claim or skill shall save:
The hero's life though Heaven denied,
   It gave our land a martyr's grave.

Nor count the teaching vainly sent
   How human hearts their griefs may share, —
The lesson woman's love has lent
   What hope may do, what faith can bear!

Farewell! the leaf-strown earth enfolds
   Our stay, our pride, our hopes, our fears;
And autumn's golden sun beholds
   A nation bowed, a world in tears.

## REJOICE.

### BY JOAQUIN MILLER.

*"Bear me out of the battle, for lo! I am sorely wounded."*

#### I.

From out my deep, wide-bosomed West,
  Where unnamed heroes hew the way
For worlds to follow, with stern zest, —
  Where gnarled old maples make array,
Deep-scarred from red men gone to rest, —
  Where pipes the quail, where squirrels play
Through tossing trees, with nuts for toy,
A boy steps forth, clear-eyed and tall,
A bashful boy, a soulful boy,
  Yet comely as the sons of Saul, —
A boy, all friendless, poor, unknown,
  Yet heir-apparent to a throne.

#### II.

Lo! Freedom's bleeding sacrifice!
  So like some tall oak tempest-blown
Beside the storied stream he lies
  Now at the last, pale-browed and prone.
A nation kneels with streaming eyes,
  A nation supplicates the throne,
A nation holds him by the hand,
  A nation sobs aloud at this:
The only dry eyes in the land
  Now at the last, I think, are his.
    Why, we should pray, God knoweth best,
    That this grand, patient soul should rest.

### III.

The world is round. The wheel has run
    Full circle. Now behold a grave
Beneath the old loved trees is done.
    The druid oaks lift up, and wave
A solemn welcome back. The brave
    Old maples murmur, every one,
"Receive him, Earth!" In centre land,
    As in the centre of each heart,
As in the hollow of God's hand,
    The coffin sinks. And with it part
        All party hates! Now, not in vain
        He bore his peril and hard pain.

### IV.

Therefore, I say, rejoice! I say,
    The lesson of his life was much, —
This boy that won, as in a day,
    The world's heart utterly; a touch
Of tenderness and tears: the page
    Of history grows rich from such;
His name the nation's heritage, —
    But oh! as some sweet angel's voice
Spake this brave death that touched us all.
    Therefore, I say, Rejoice! Rejoice!
        Run high the flags! Put by the pall!
        Lo! all is for the best for all!

## SONNET — JAMES A. GARFIELD.

#### BY REV. H. BERNARD CARPENTER.

Lo! as a pure, white statue wrought with care
  By some strong hand, which moulds from Life and Death
  Beauty more beautiful than blood or breath,
And straight 'tis veiled; and, whilst all men repair
To see this wonder in the workshop, there!
  Behold, it gleams unveiled to curious eye
  Far-seen, high-placed in Art's pale gallery,
Where all stand mute before a work so fair:
So he, our man of men, in vision stands,
  With Pain and Patience crowned imperial;
    Death's veil has dropped; far from this house of woe
He hears one love-chant out of many lands,
  Whilst from his mystic noon-height he lets fall
    His shadow o'er these hearts that bleed below.
SEPT. 26, 1881.

## MIDNIGHT.

#### SEPTEMBER 19, 1881.

#### BY JOHN BOYLE O'REILLY.

ONCE in a lifetime we may see the veil
  Tremble and lift, that hides symbolic things;
The spirit's vision, when the senses fail,
  Sweeps the weird meaning that the outlook brings.

Deep in the midst of turmoil, it may be, —
  A crowded street, a forum, or a field, —
The soul inverts the telescope, to see
  To-day's event in future years revealed.

Back from the present, let us look at Rome ;
    Now, see what Cato meant, what Brutus said.
Hark ! the Athenians welcome Cimon home !
    — How clear they are, those glimpses of the dead !

But we, hard toilers, we who plan and weave
    Through common days the web of common life,
What word, alas ! shall teach us to receive
    The mystic meaning of our peace and strife ?

Whence comes our symbol ? Surely God must speak ;
    No less than he can make us heed or pause :
Self-seekers we, too busy or too weak
    To search beyond our daily lives and laws.

'Gainst things occult our earth-turned eyes rebel ;
    No sound of Destiny can reach our ears ;
We have no time for dreaming — Hark ! a knell, —
    A knell at midnight ! All the nation hears !

A second grievous throb ! The dreamers wake ;
    The merchant's soul forgets his goods and ships ;
The humble workmen from their slumbers break ;
    The women raise their eyes with quivering lips ;

The miner rests upon his pick to hear :
    The printer's type stops midway from the case ;
The solemn sound has reached the roisterer's ear,
    And brought the shame and sorrow to his face.

Again it booms ! Oh, mystic veil, upraise !
    — Behold, 'tis lifted ! On the darkness drawn,
A picture, lined with light ! The people's gaze,
    From sea to sea, beholds it till the dawn :

A death-bed scene, — a sinking sufferer lies,
    Their chosen ruler, crowned with love and pride ;
Around, his counsellors, with streaming eyes ;
    His wife heart-broken, kneeling by his side :

Death's shadow holds her; it will pass too soon;
    She weeps in silence — bitterest of tears;
He wanders softly — Nature's kindest boon,
    And as he whispers all the country hears.

For him the pain is past, the struggle ends:
    His cares and honors fade: his younger life
In peaceful Mentor comes, with dear old friends;
    His mother's arms take home his sweet young wife;

He stands among the students, tall and strong,
    And teaches truths republican and grand:
He moves — ah, pitiful! — he sweeps along,
    O'er fields of carnage leading his command!

He speaks to crowded faces; round him surge
    Thousands and millions of excited men:
He hears them cheer, sees some great light emerge,
    Is borne as on a tempest: then — ah, then!

The fancies fade, the fever's work is past;
    A moment's pang — then recollections thrill:
He feels the faithful lips that kiss their last.
    His heart beats once in answer, and is still!

The curtain falls; but hushed, as if afraid,
    The people wait, tear-stained, with heaving breast;
'Twill rise again, they know, when he is laid
    With Freedom, in the Capitol, at rest.

Once more they see him, in his coffin, there,
    As Lincoln lay in blood-stained martyr sleep;
The stars and stripes across his honored bier.
    While Freedom and Columbia o'er him weep.

## "HE IS DEAD, OUR PRESIDENT."

### BY CHARLES TURNER DAZEY.

[THE HARVARD CLASS POET OF 1881.]

HE is dead, our President; he rests in an honored grave,
He whom any one of us would gladly have died to save.
All is over at last, the long, brave struggle for life, —
For a nation's sake, not his own, and for that of children and wife.
Doubt and suspense are dead; dead is the passionate thrill
Of a hope too blessed and sweet for aught but death to kill.
Do you remember yet, how, from that awful day
When the pulse of the nation stopped with a shock of wild dismay,
And voiceless horror looked from questioning eyes to eyes,
As the murmur widened and spread, "Our President murdered lies," —
How to the very last, like a star in a night of gloom,
The hope of the people burned till it sank in a hero's tomb?
*We could not give him up:* as a mother prays for her child,
We prayed for his precious life, with a love as deep and wild.
We had known him long and well as a man of royal mind,
Who had nobly proved his birthright as a leader of mankind.
We had watched him, oh, so proudly! as in life's ranks he rose
By the fair and open warfare that endeared him to his foes:
But we never prized him rightly until he had meekly lain
Wrapped in speechless tortures of the fiery furnace of pain.
Then how we learned to love him! for all that man holds dear,
For infinite faith and patience, and courage when death drew near,
For yearning love that strove with a pitiful, mighty strife,
To shield from the sting of sorrow the hearts of mother and wife.
Then with tearful vision, purged of passion and pride,
We saw in its tender beauty that spirit glorified;
And mighty love swept o'er us with a current as deep and grand
As the Nile that swells to a sea to nourish a hungry land.

O boundless sea of love, and star of a hope that is dead,
Not vainly our President died, not vainly our loved one bled,
If still that sea shall sweep onward which at first so narrow ran
Till the hands of the nations clasp in the brotherhood of man,
Till the hate that smoulders still in hearts unreconciled
Shall change to the sweet affection that beams in the glance of a child,
And gladness shall dawn from sorrow, and glory burst from gloom.
And the flower of love fraternal shall blossom from Garfield's tomb.

CAMBRIDGE, MASS., Sept. 25, 1881.

## J. A. G.

### BY JULIA WARD HOWE.

Our sorrow sends its shadow round the earth.
So brave, so true! A hero from his birth!
The plumes of Empire moult, in mourning draped,
The lightning's message by our tears is shaped.

Life's vanities that blossom for an hour
Heap on his funeral car their fleeting flower.
Commerce forsakes her temples, blind and dim,
And pours her tardy gold, to homage him.

The notes of grief to age familiar grow
Before the sad privations all must know;
But the majestic cadence which we hear
To-day, is new in either hemisphere.

What crown is this, high hung and hard to reach,
Whose glory so outshines our laboring speech?
The crown of Honor, pure and unbetrayed;
He wins the spurs who bears the knightly aid.

While royal babes incipient empire hold,
And, for bare promise, grasp the sceptre's gold,
This man such service to his age did bring
That they who knew him servant, hailed him king.

In poverty his infant couch was spread ;
His tender hands soon wrought for daily bread ;
But from the cradle's bound his willing feet
The errand of the moment went to meet.

When learning's page unfolded to his view,
The quick disciple straight a teacher grew ;
And, when the fight of freedom stirred the land,
Armed was his heart and resolute his hand.

Wise in the council, stalwart in the field !
Such rank supreme a workman's hut may yield.
His onward steps like measured marbles show,
Climbing the height where God's great flame doth glow.

Ah ! Rose of joy, that hid'st a thorn so sharp !
Ah ! Golden woof that meet'st a severed warp !
Ah ! Solemn comfort that the stars rain down !
The hero's garland his, the martyr's crown !

NEWPORT, Sept. 25, 1881.

## FATHERLESS.

### BY KATE TANNATT WOODS.

OVER the land the tidings sped,
"The leader has fallen, our chief is dead ; "
And over the land a cry of pain
Began and ended with Garfield's name.

"He is dead," said each, with tearful eye:
"So strong, so true, why must he die?"
And the children paused that autumn day
To talk of the good man passed away.

Over the land, when the tidings came,
Even the babies lisped his name;
And youthful eyes grew sad that day
For the fatherless children far away.

Fatherless. — word with a life of pain;
Fatherless, — never complete again;
Always to miss, and never to know,
The joy of his greeting, — his love below.

Missing the cheerful smile each day,
Missing his care in studies or play,
Missing each hour, each day, each year,
The sound of a voice so tender and dear.

Fatherless! only the children can tell
The sound of that dreary funeral knell;
For only they, in all coming years,
Find the roses of youth bedewed with tears.

Over the land, from shore to shore,
The prayer of the children is echoed o'er, —
"God of the fatherless, help, we pray,
The wards of our mourning nation to-day."

**Salem**, Sept. 24, 1881.

## LAUREL — CYPRESS.

BY LOUISA PARSONS HOPKINS.
[AUTHOR OF "MOTHERHOOD."]

*MARCH 4, 1881.*

HE stands at the Capitol's portal
　　With lifted hand.
The vows of God are upon him
　　For the trust of the land;
　　Chief true and grand!

His manhood turns in its glory
　　To womanhood.
To his wife and mother he yearns
　　From the multitude;
　　Heart true and good!

He crowns them before the people
　　With kiss of love.
See it, ye men, and shout, —
　　Full hearts will out;
　　Rend the heavens above!

*SEPTEMBER 23, 1881.*

He lies in the wide rotunda,
　　With folded palms;
"Wounded for our transgressions."
　　Comrades in arms,
　　Spread ye his pall,
　　For the peace of all!

The thronging crowds have passed him,
　　With falling tear;
A queenly woman's garland
　　Upon his bier;
　　Knight without fear,
　　Man brave and dear!

In this his martyr-glory
   Leave him alone;
For his kiss-crowned wife is coming.
   Though dead, he has known
   She would come — his own —
   To share his throne.

NEW BEDFORD, Sept. 26, 1881.

## THE LAST BULLETIN.

### BY MARIE E. BLAKE.

DAY after day as morning skies did flame,
  "How fares our liege?" we cried with eager breath, —
  "How fares our liege, who fights the fight with death?"
And ever with fresh hope the answer came;

Until that solemn midnight when the clang
  Of woeful bells tolled out their tale of dread,
  That he, the good and gifted one, was dead,
And through his weeping land the message rang.

Then in the darkness every heart was bowed:
  While thinking on the direful ways of Fate,
  Where Love could thus be overthrown by Hate, —
"So wrong hath conquered right!" we said aloud.

"If this be life, what matter how it flies;
  What strength or power or glory crowns a name;
  What noble meed of honesty or fame,
Since all these gifts were his, — and there he lies

Blighted by malice! Woe's the day! and dead
  While yet the fields of his most golden prime
  Are rich in all the pomp of summer-time,
With all their ripening wealth unharvested!"

. . . . . . . . .

Thus fares it with our liege? Nay, doubting soul,
Not thus; but grandly raised to nobler height
Of strength and power and most divine delight,
— At one swift breath made beautiful and whole!

Nor mocked by broken hope, or shattered plan,
By some pale ghost of duty left undone,
By haunting moments wasted one by one,
But crowned with that which best becometh man.

Holding with brimming hands his heart's desire;
While the fierce light of these last glorious days,
Blazing on each white line of thought and ways,
Touches his record with immortal fire!

BOSTON, Sept. 25, 1881.

## J. A. G.

### HUMANITAS REGNANS.

#### BY M. J. SAVAGE.

WITH finger on lip, and breath bated,
With an eager and sad desire,
The world stood hushed, as it waited
For the click of the fateful wire.

"*Better:*" and civilization
Breathed freer and hoped again.
"*Worse:*" and through every nation
Went throbbing a thrill of pain.

A cry at midnight! and listening —
"*Dead!*" tolled out the bells of despair;
And millions of eyelids were glistening
As sobbed the sad tones on the air.

But who is he toward whom all eyes are turning?
And who is he for whom all hearts are yearning?

What is the threat at which earth holds its breath
While one lone man a duel fights with death?

---

No thrones are hanging in suspense;
   No kingdoms totter to their fall.
Peace, with her gentle influence,
   Is hovering over all.

'Tis just one man at Elberon,
   Who waiteth day by day,
Whose patience all our hearts hath won
   As ebbs his life away.

His birthday waked no cannon-boom;
   No purple round him hung:
A backwoods cabin gave him room;
   And storms his welcome sung.

He seized the sceptre of that king
   Who treads a freehold sod:
He wore upon his brow that ring
   That crowns a son of God.

By his own might he built a throne,
   With no unhuman arts,
And by his manhood reigned alone
   O'er fifty million hearts.

Thus is humanity's long dream,
   Its highest, holiest hope, begun
To harden into fact, and gleam
   A city 'neath the sun. —

A city, not like that which came
   In old-time vision from the skies;
But wrought by man through blood and flame,
   From solid earth to rise, —

Man's city; the ideal reign
   Where every human right hath place;
Where blood, nor birth, nor priest again
   Shall bind the weary race, —

*In which no king but man shall be.*
   'Twas this that thrilled with loving pain
The heart of all the earth, as he
   Died by the sobbing main.

For, mightiest ruler of the earth,
   He was the mightiest, not because
Of priestly touch, or blood, or birth,
   But by a people's laws.

---

O Garfield! brave and patient soul!
Long as the tireless tides shall roll
About the *Long Branch* beaches, where
Thy life went out upon the air,
So long thy land, from sea to sea,
Will hold thy manhood's legacy.

There *were* two parties: there were those,
In thine own party, called thy foes;
There *was* a North; there *was* a South,
Ere blazed the assassin's pistol-mouth.

But lo! thy bed became a throne;
   And, as the hours went by, at length
The weakness of thine arm alone
   Grew mightier than thy strongest strength.

No petulant murmur; no vexed cry
Of balked ambitions; but a high,
Grand patience! And thy whisper blent
In one heart all the continent.
To-day there are no factions left,
But *one America* bereft.

---

O Garfield! fortunate in death wast thou,
　　Though at the opening of a grand career!
Thou wast a meteor flashing on the brow
　　Of skies political, where oft appear,

And disappear, so many stars of promise. Then,
　　While all men watched thy high course, wondering
If thou wouldst upward sweep, or fall again,
　　Thee from thine orbit mad hands thought to fling;

And lo! the meteor, with its fitful light,
　　All on a sudden stood, and was a star, —
A radiance fixed, to glorify the night
　　There where the world's proud constellations are.

---

## JAMES ABRAM GARFIELD.

### BY FRANCIS A. NICHOLS.

O GOLDEN-ROD upon the hill!
　　O white-lipped lily of the lake!
No longer bloom to half fulfil
　　A promise made for promise' sake!
Let brambles grow, let thistles blow:
What careth he? He cannot know.

O waving fields of ripening grain!
   O fruitage of the vine and tree!
Nor kissing sun nor soothing rain
   Again shall wake maturity.
No seed may grow; no man may sow.
What careth he? He cannot know.

O breast of woman! bearing pain
   To round the fulness of thy life:
No first low cry of babe again
   Shall meet the ear of prayerful wife.
No mother's love; no mother's woe.
What careth he? He cannot know.

O sun! O moon! O stars! O day!
   Forever vanished from our sight!
Nor love nor faith may find a ray
   For guidance from eternal night:
The light may come: the light may go.
What careth he? He cannot know.

O grave! beneath some clouded sky,
   Low-lurking near his hallowed head,
Henceforth, nor mourning robe nor sigh
   Shall know the living from the dead.
What though our hearts shall fill and flow?
What careth he? He cannot know.

O harp attuned to holy things!
   Forbear, in grief, to lose the strain. —
The grand old strain the prophet sings, —
   "The dead shall rise to life again!"
Thus life will come; thus life will go.
'Tis well! for God hath ordered so.

## "'TIS O'ER AT LAST."

### BY JOSEPH W. NYE.

'Tis o'er at last — the doubtful strife,
   We watched so long in hope and fear.
The die is cast! With sadness rife
   We gather at our ruler's bier.

The starry flag o'er all the land
   The story sad at half-mast tells;
Sounds solemnly on every hand
   The mournful requiem of bells.

No faction breaks the grief wide-spread;
   No State or section stands apart:
All join in mourning for him dead;
   He finds a place in every heart.

The thrilling words he often spake,
   With eloquence almost divine,
All patriotic hearts awake,
   From the Palmetto to the Pine!

What though our prayers did not avail,
   The suffering, prostrate form to raise?
Our trust in God will never fail,
   We cannot cease his name to praise.

"God reigns!" His purpose underlies
   The weak designs of finite man;
The plots which scheming men devise
   Can never thwart his wondrous plan.

He ever makes man's wrath to praise
   His overruling power and love,
Thus bringing men to know his ways,
   And drawing them to heaven above.

Columbia weeps not alone;
    The world partakes the heavy woe:
From cot to cot, from throne to throne,
    The streams of grief and sorrow flow.

Lo, England's Queen (God bless her!) sends
    Her tribute of esteem sincere,
Which with a thousand offerings blends
    To crown the martyr's hallowed bier!

The generations yet unborn
    Will oft the tearful story tell,
How, on that fated summer morn,
    The noble form of GARFIELD fell!

Patient and calm through trials long
    Of weariness and ceaseless pain,
The victim of a deed of wrong
    To be repeated ne'er again!

Against the hand that laid him low,
    We heard from *him* nor wrath nor hate,
But *million* hearts impatient grow
    To mete the murderer his fate!

What are the bays which warriors crown?
    The spurs of gold by knighthood won?
His were the honor and renown
    Of *manhood true* and *duty done*.

Our noble leader, living still,
    Is "marching on" to duties new,
His noble mission to fulfil
    The spirit's subtile influence through!

Rest, patriot, in thy narrow bed,
    While flowers we culled bedeck thy mound:
A brighter crown adorns thy head,
    Where joys supernal e'er abound.

LYNN, MASS.

# POEMS WRITTEN FOR OTHER PAPERS.

## ELBERON.

### BY J. W. TURNER.

[From The East Boston Advocate.]

#### I.

'Twas eventide: the stars were beaming from on high,
The balmy breeze of autumn gently floated by,
As at my casement gazing out upon
The world, my thoughts were still at Elberon.

#### II.

List! dost thou hear that sound — that mournful knell?
Those tones that vibrate over hill and dell?
From east to west upon this midnight calm,
From north to south — oh, hear the sad alarm!

#### III.

Ah, yes! a nation's tears too plainly tell
Too well, alas! to us, what has befell,
And hope, once cherished in our hearts, has fled, —
Our President, our noble Garfield's dead!

#### IV.

O sad Columbia! stricken land, for thee
This hour of solemn grief's dark destiny!
The tidings now so fraught with gloom and pain
That's lingering o'er thy great and wide domain.

#### V.

O God! we turn our inmost thoughts above,
Invoke thy aid, — thy ever tender love;
For by thy will, thy might, and thy command,
Is life, is love, is home and native land.

### VI.

O wife bereft! O aged mother dear!
O darling children in affliction drear!
A nation bears her sympathy to thee,
This hour of death, — of death's great mystery.

### VII.

Oh! teach the ones, those men who high in state,
All noble deeds of good to emulate,
And stay the bold and base assassin's way,
Whose hand uplifted would a mortal slay.

### VIII.

O thou lamented, loved of all thy race!
From boy to man thy nobleness we trace :
All hearts are beating sadly, tenderly ;
A nation's tears are falling now for thee.

### IX.

Too soon, alas! the portals of the grave
Will ope for thee, thou noble, good, and brave;
But yet around thee in that sacred shrine,
Oh! millions will their purest love intwine.

EAST BOSTON, September, 1881.

---

## REST, NOBLE CHIEF.

### BY C. D. BRADLEE.

[From The Boston Advertiser.]

REST, noble chief, and sweetly rest:
Thy work is done, God's will is best.
A faithful life is finished now:
The seal of death is on thy brow.

Rise, noble chief, rise up to heaven:
Another life our God has given;
And angel robes are thine by right,
And all thy days shall now be bright.

Take now thy crown, beloved of all,
And hear our God's approving call;
Whilst we on earth bow low, and weep,
*And sad and lonely vigils keep.*

## A TOUCHING SONNET.

### BY ERIC S. ROBERTSON.

[From The New York Herald.]

The following sonnet was written in St. Paul's Cathedral, London, after the funeral anthem for President Garfield had been sung: —

*September 25.*

Through tears to look upon a tearful crowd,
  And hear the anthem echoing
  High in the dome till angels seem to fling
The chant of England up through vault and cloud,
Making ethereal register aloud
  At Heaven's own gate. It was a sorrowing
  To make a good man's death seem such a thing
As makes imperial purple of his shroud.

Some creeds there be like runes we cannot spell,
  And some like stars that flicker in their flame;
But some so clear the sun scarce shines so well;
  For when with Moses' touch a dead man's name
Finds tears within strange rocks as this name can,
We know right well that God was with the man.

---

## THE MIDNIGHT OF A NATION.

### BY CHARLOTTE FISKE BATES.

[From The Boston Transcript.]

Thirty-eight! counted the solemn stroke
In as many a solemn minute!
At the second or third the hardiest folk
The spell of their midnight revel broke;
The hum of pleasure, the groan of care,
Sank to a hushed grief everywhere, —
And the still heaven had anguish in it!

O States! whatever ye were before,
Be *one* for an endless morrow!
Thirty and eight! from the very core
Of the nation's soul doth her grief outpour,
In this deep of Death's and Nature's dark.
One anguish in thirty-eight breathings, hark!
All one, all one, in the orphan's sorrow.

## AN ODE ON THE ASSASSINATION.

[A prize offered by a London weekly for the best poem on the attempted assassination of President Garfield was awarded to the author of the following.]

VEIL now, O Liberty! thy blushing face,
   At the fell deed that thrills a startled world;
While fair Columbia weeps in dire disgrace,
   And bows in sorrow o'er the banner furled.

No graceless tyrant falls by vengeance here,
   'Neath the wild justice of a secret knife;
No red Ambition ends its grim career,
   And expiates its horrors with its life.

Not here does rash Revenge misguided burn,
   To free a nation with the assassin's dart;
Or roused Despair in angry madness turn,
   And tear its freedom from a despot's heart.

But where blest Liberty so widely reigns,
   And Peace and Plenty mark a smiling land,
Here the mad wretch its fair white record stains
   And blurs its beauties with a "bloody hand."

Here the elect of millions, and the pride
   Of those who own his mild and peaceful rule, —
Here virtue sinks and yields the crimson tide,
   Beneath the vile unreason of a fool!

---

## THE DEAD PRESIDENT.

### BY J. G. HOLLAND.

A WASP flew out upon our fairest son,
And stung him to the quick with poisoned shaft,
The while he chatted carelessly, and laughed,
And knew not of the fateful mischief done.
And so this life amid our love begun,
Envenomed by the insect's hellish craft,
Was drunk by Death in one long feverish draught,
And he was lost, — our precious, priceless one.

Oh, mystery of blind, remorseless fate!
Oh, cruel end of a most causeless hate,
That life so mean should murder life so great!
What is there left to us who think and feel,
Who have no remedy and no appeal,
But damn the wasp, and crush him under heel?

---

## IN PACE REQUIESCAT.

[From Frank Leslie's Illustrated Newspaper.]

### I.

Hush, hush! speak softly!
The conflict now has reached the end:
  Life lies vanquished on the ground;
  Death with victor's wreath is crowned.
O angels, stoop! O God, defend!

### II.

Toll, toll, toll, toll,
Ye brazen bells of woe and dread!
  Thy requiem send throughout all lands,
  Sweep on to distant ocean strands:
He lieth silent, — lieth dead.

### III.

Gather, gather, clouds,
O darkest clouds of sombre night!
  Lock the golden, smiling stars
  Safe behind thy prison-bars:
Grief wisheth not, nor beareth light.

### IV.

Droop, droop, Freedom's flag!
Float not thy folds majestic, proud;
  Lie thou still across the breast
  Of him the country loveth best:
It is a well-befitting shroud.

### V.

Yet, O Columbia! free, —
Up from the past there rings the cry:
  "God reigns — the Government still lives!"
  In the nation's heart, that honor gives,
He "only sleeps," he *cannot die.*

## SEPTEMBER NINETEENTH.

### BY L. M. S.

[From The Boston Transcript.]

Toll! toll! ye solemn midnight bells!
From spire to spire the thrilling echo swells;
And to our hearts the mournful story tells, —
    Gone! Gone! Gone!

Millions of watchers list with bated breath
To iron tongues that tell our martyr's death.
"Is this the end?" each to another saith, —
    Gone! Gone! Gone!

Is this the outcome of our prayers and tears?
The harvest of his honest toil of years
Buoyed by strong faith, and ne'er a prey to fears? —
    Gone! Gone! Gone!

And has it ended with the assassin's blow?
Why has it been permitted so?
We feel that only God can know.
    Gone! Gone! Gone!

A finished life! More perfect in its plan
Than would have been devised by man,
Perfected only as God can.
    Gone! Gone! Gone!

Had he remained upon the chair of state,
He scarcely could escape the fate —
Envy and misjudgment — which attends the great.
    Now gone! Gone! Gone!

But his sublime patience on a bed of pain
Has bound all hearts as with an iron chain:
He has not suffered thus in vain,
    Though gone! Gone!

What richer gift could bless him from above
Than the whole nation's undivided love?
Without one voice that will dissenting prove,
    Now he is gone!

His upright life has stood each crucial test,
His *living* every mortal blest,
His saintly death completes the rest.
  Gone! Gone! Gone!

No more his voice a guiding star can be;
But his great soul lives in eternity,
And his pure life is a reality,
  Though gone.

Like the ripe sheaf that is cut and bound,
Homeward along its path is found,
Broadcast, rich grain upon the ground;

So all along the path he moved
Are found in the hearts of those he loved
Rare memories which his goodness proved.

The words that all our hearts have thrilled
Are ours; though the great heart is stilled,
And the soul with noble motives filled
  Is gone! Gone! Gone!

Again our chieftain's voice we hear:
As the sad tolling falls upon our ear,
The calling seemeth very near, —
  Come! Come! Come!

Like the bell's home, the tower high,
His life points upward to the sky:
To his heart heaven was always nigh.
  Come! Come! Come!

God heard our prayers, not as we would:
His great love better understood,
And answered as a Father should.
  Gone! Gone! Gone!

Weep, strong men! ye have lost a friend!
With heads uncovered to your Maker bend!
  *He* fashioned that great soul,
  He destined this great end.

## JAMES A. GARFIELD.

### BY GEORGE A. PARKHURST.

[From The Lowell Weekly Journal.]

Rest, hero, rest! Earth's pains are o'er:
  Thy greatest triumph has been won,
As, echoing from heaven's golden door,
  We seem to hear, "Servant, well done!"

Rest, hero, rest! For thee no more
  The tortured frame, the fevered brow;
But on eternity's bright shore
  The peace of God is with thee now.

Rest, hero, rest! Secure thy fame
  Among the pure, the good, the great:
Time's record bears no nobler name
  Of those who served their God and State.

Rest, hero, rest! While round thy bier
  Columbia's sons are bending low,
No clime but drops the mourner's tear,
  No land but shares the common woe.

Rest, brother, rest! In this sad hour
  We seek thy throne, Father divine:
Though clouds of sorrow round us lower,
  Teach us to have no will but thine.

CHELMSFORD, MASS., Sept. 22, 1881.

---

## TOLL THE BELLS GENTLY.

### BY D. GILBERT DEXTER.

[From The Cambridge Tribune.]

Toll the bells gently! Garfield is dead!
The nation is weeping a noble son slain:
It may be his equal we'll ne'er see again.
  Toll the bells gently! Hope has not fled.

Toll the bells gently! Toll them with care!
"Great heart" is bleeding, and mourning her son,
Whose greatness and goodness the world's homage won.
  Toll the bells gently! Toll them with care!

Toll the bells gently! But never despair!
The nation still lives: her sons may depart
Ne'er to return — let the living take heart.
  Toll the bells gently! Toll them with care!

Toll the bells gently! From Elberon's shore
There cometh a message to daughter and son
That "God knoweth best" how the victory's won.
  Toll the bells gently! The struggle is o'er!

Toll the bells gently! From Washington home;
Bind up the hearts that are breaking in grief;
God of our fathers, oh bring sweet relief!
  Toll the bells gently! In bearing him home!

Toll the bells gently! The noble one's slain!
On Erie's blest shore, near the home he loved best,
Lay him to rest, brothers, lay him to rest.
  Toll the bells gently! Toll them gently again!

---

## OUR DEAD PRESIDENT.

[From The Boston Commonwealth.]

THE dreaded news has come at last.
  Far o'er the land the tidings roll:
The lingering life from us has past,
  And grief and anguish fill our soul.

We watched, with tender care and true,
  These long, long weeks of suffering keen:
Our hopes and prayers around him grew,
  That better days would yet be seen.

For, as the sun at times will dart
  Through clouds that threaten all the day,
So gleams of hope for us would start,
  And make us trust the fuller ray.

But now we know the night has come;
  The orb has set we loved so well:
The patriot finds the heavenly home
  Where all true souls in union dwell.

His life was done. The power yet lives
   That builds a nation true and wise;
And God, in his sad dying, gives
   A morning promise to our skies.

For shall we not more faithful be
   To this Republic, torn and crost,
And place her foremost of the free,
   That nothing to mankind be lost?

And shall we not to her accord
   A service perfect, wise, and true,
And help along his good life-word,
   And in our lives his own renew?

---

## THE MIDNIGHT KNELL.

### BY HENRY C. DANE.

[From The Boston Transcript.]

I SAT at the hour of midnight,
   Weary and sad and lone,
In fancy watching the lamplight
   That from the sick-room shone;
While a silence deep and solemn
   Brooded over the earth, —
The silence attending the column
   Of angels — leading Death!

The heart of Nature seemed throbbing
   With pity, pain, and woe,
As it watched a nation sobbing
   With anguish deep and low,
While it waited and hoped with fear
   The tidings at the dawn, —
The tidings it dreaded to hear
   From that cot at Elberon!

Once more I perused the message, —
   "*It still looks very dark!*"
And thought of that noble visage
   That lay in Elberon's — Hark!
Out from the towering steeple,
   Breaking the weary spell,
Came the message to the people, —
   The deep, the midnight knell!

"Gone!" "Gone!" it rang, — that doleful bell,
  From spire and dome and tower,
Crushing a nation with its knell, —
  That awful midnight hour!
On, on it rolled o'er distant West,
  Through valleys broad and deep,
Waking a nation from its rest,
  To bow with grief, and weep.

Daughter heroic, and mother,
  Your tortures who dare tell, —
There without son and brother,
  By him you loved so well.
A nation holds you to its heart,
  And hold you will forever:
It shares with you the bitter part;
  Its love nought e'er can sever.

Gone! gone! our hero-chieftain gone!
  Struck in his hour of might,
And falling o'er his work undone,
  Because he dared the right.
O people boasting of thy power!
  O nation just begun!
Learn thy lesson from this sad hour,
  And see thy duty done!

Gaze on that form so tried and torn;
  Gaze on that deep-scarred face:
There learn the lesson not yet won, —
  The duties ye must face!
O men of honor, truth, and power!
  O men of mighty zeal!
Step to the front in this dark hour,
  And help our woes to heal!

From Vernon's deep and silent shade,
  From Marshfield's solemn shore,
From Oakland's calm and peaceful glade,
  And all the broad land o'er,
From those who sleep in patriot graves,
  The warning voice is heard, —
"This is your hour! be men, not slaves!
  *Redeem our plighted word!*"

BOSTON, Sept. 20, 1881.

## "THE PRESIDENT IS DEAD!"

### BY S. V. A.

[From The Boston Home Journal.]

Gone in his fair and manly prime;
Gone in his faith and hope sublime;
Gone when his feet had climbed so high,
No step remained but to the sky;
Then on earth's topmost round, his ear
Caught greetings from the upper sphere,
And angel voices whispered, "Come!
Thy work is done! come home! come home!"
"I'm ready; I'm content," he said;
And while the stricken nation plead
In words of agonizing prayer,
That God her ruler's life might spare,
He with a calm, unfaltering heart,
Waited until the poisoned dart
Should end its mission, whether life
In realms above, or toil and strife
Below might be his lot, and still
Submissive, bowed unto the Will
That holds the nations in His hand,
And at whose word they fall or stand.
O Garfield! President beloved!
Ruler and statesman, tried and proved,
We write thy name among earth's peers,
We send it down the coming years,
Wreathed with rich honors, memories proud,
Of courage ne'er by evil cowed,
Of patriot deed, and lofty aim—
We crown it with immortal fame,
And unto thousands yet unborn
The heritage we leave, that, shorn
Of all dishonor, they may tread
The rugged path of duty, led
By thine example, chaste and pure
As those who martyrdom endure.
We mourn for thee with falling tears;
Our bosoms swell with rising fears;
With grievous wounds our spirits bleed.
O Father! in this hour of need,
Be with our country: may the rod
Of chastening, watered with the blood

Of this most noble victim, bloom
With flowers that even o'er his tomb
Shall shed such odorous sweets, that not
In vain the sacrifice, the blot
That crimson stains our lovely land
From Eastern unto Western strand.
May such a band of heroes rise,
So loyal, temperate, true, and wise,
So just, alike to friends and foes,
That his pure life, and e'en its close,
Shall bear, though grief now makes it mute,
A harvest of immortal fruit.

SEPT. 19, 1881.

---

## "GOD GRANT HIM PEACE."

### BY ANNA FORD PIPER.

[From The Boston Transcript.]

Low lies our noble dead,
Who for his country bled.
    God grant him peace!
With each new morning's ray,
And 'mid the toil of day,
Father, to thee we pray,
    . God grant him peace!

Gone is our guiding hand,
Gone to the silent land,
    Gone evermore!
Yet while enthroned on high,
Christ reigns in majesty,
Father, to thee we cry,
    God grant him peace!

Pure, noble, just, and free,
Still may our nation be,
    Father, we pray.
May we through darkest night,
Led by thy beacon light,
Like him defend the right.
    God grant him peace!

## JAMES A. GARFIELD.

### BY EMMA POMEROY EATON.

[From The Boston Transcript.]

O SWEET and patient soul, enduring, bold!
Thy rare, ennobling virtues were not told
Until, sore stricken by no fault of thine,
A waiting world beheld thy strength divine.

Hast thou not honor, when from east to west
The whole world round obeys one sad behest?
Prone at thy bier a sorrowing people lies,
And each with all in lowly homage vies.

O noble one and true! thou canst not die.
Throned in the nation's heart, thou liv'st for aye:
Thine aim and purpose shall thy life outrun,
Nor aim and purpose die, though life be done.

CAMBRIDGE, Sept. 23, 1881.

---

## GARFIELD DEAD.

### BY D. P.

[From The Capital.]

"Duncan is in his grave:
After life's fitful fever he sleeps well.
Treason has done his worst; nor steel, nor poison,
Malice domestic, foreign levy, nothing
Can touch him further." — *Shakspeare.*

HURT unto death, and dead at last. In vain
The cry of anguish from the people wrung,
That like a tender mother tearful hung,
    In grief sublime,
Counting by pulse-beats the fatal steps of time
    Above that bed of pain.
The land was dark with sorrow. From wooded Maine
To where the wide Pacific chafes the Golden Gate,
From blue North lakes down to the Flowery State,
From cities, hamlets, mountain, glen and plain,
    E'en from the wilderness,
Wherever a human heart has beat, or human footstep trod,
    Went up to God

The cry for succor in our sore distress.
    The fearful rent,
That internecine war wrought us in twain,
  His precious blood is God's cement,
To bind us in one brotherhood again.
Grief washed out Passion's angry hue,
And mingling tears for him come gray and blue.
    In vain
May selfish factions seek once more to reign,
    And stir to life
Our evil passions into bloody strife,
That once our nation's hopes in common ruin blent.
Land whispered unto land. Beneath the solemn main,
  Through dark, unfathomed caves, the lightning-laden nerve of life
For an instant trembled with our tale of pain,
  And nations paused, amid their vexing strife,
To send their sorrow back to us again.
Crowned heads were bowed; and back-bent toil,
Watering with unrequited sweat the alien soil,
    With uncovered head,
Stood in the presence of our mighty dead.
The dead have lain in state,
The wise, the good, the great, —
Soldier, statesman, potentate, —
And o'er the land, to grief awake,
Huge bells swinging to and fro,
    Solemn and slow,
With iron tongues have told their tales of woe,
While waves of music beat upon the air
In rhythmed sweetness all their wild despair.
It was our living that we laid in state:
    And the nation, desolate,
Through the heavy watches with breath abate:
And hearts nigh broken praying for the balm
Of health again; for on that quickening breath
And fever-hurried face rode Death.
Ah! not for him alone: we saw with dread
The Great Republic hanging by a slender thread;
    And he alone was calm.
Patient and brave, as gentle as a child,
    He sadly smiled,
While grief around was wild,
And took the chance they gave him. Tender and true,
How sweet and homely were his words of cheer,
In answer to his poor wife's tears and fear,

"Don't cry, sweetheart: we will yet pull through."
What recks all glory to that lonely home,
Where sits the mother, aged and alone?
Of all, alas! bereft, sad she sits, and dreams
      Upon life's earlier scenes, —
Of the hard struggle and her noble son,
Who fought through all until the goal was won;
And in the hour of triumph, with loving grace,
Turned to kiss her in the nation's place.
      She cannot feel him dead:
His manly form and noble head
  Are ever with her; he's "her baby" still.
The dim perceptions cloud the present o'er,
  And save the pains that kill.
The broken rainbow yet its arch retains,
And points to earth like life. Our grave remains,
Whatever glory be for us in store.

God help the brave, true heart
  That lost not hope till hope itself was dead, —
The loving wife, who filled an angel's part,
  And smiled to cheer above a heart that bled;
Who crowded down the blinding tears
    And anguished fears,
    Hiding her pain,
That she alone might nurse her lord to life again.
  Our hero's widow is a nation's care,
    Her babes the people's own.
    Ah, me! of what avail the groan,
    The lamentations all must share?
Vain mockery of words. They deeper grief will start
To one who carries dead like this upon her living heart.
    Thou art gone;
And the great world goes roaring on, —
The cities hum of human life, the roar
Of ocean on the rocky shore;
Season follows season; and o'er the land,
In sun and storm, the farmer's horny hand
Tills the warm earth;
Myriads of men have birth,
And myriads are carried to the tomb;
Birds sing, and flowers bloom,
And shining rivers roll in music to the sea:
No more, no more; oh! never more may we
Turn in our love to thee.

We search in vain,
By mountain side, or lake, or plain,
Or thy loved solitude
Of thought-haunted wood,
Or rocky glen,
Or 'mid the busy haunts of men:
No more may we our hero see.
Thy kingly form is mouldering into dust;
Thy spirit is with God, we trust;
Thy life has passed into a memory.

MAC-O-CHEE, 21st September, 1881.

---

## REQUIEM.

### BY H. L. HASTINGS.

[From The Boston Journal.]

Toll, toll the bells!
The midnight silence waking.
Toll, toll the bells!
The nation's heart is breaking.

Toll, toll the bells!
Nor tarry till the morrow.
Toll, toll the bells!
That voice a nation's sorrow.

Toll, toll the bells!
A stricken widow weepeth.
Toll, toll the bells!
A wearied sufferer sleepeth.

Toll, toll the bells!
Now to thy knees, O nation!
Toll, toll the bells!
In God is thy salvation.

Toll, toll the bells!
The solemn memory cherish.
One man has died,[1]
Let not the nation perish!

CHELSEA, Midnight, Sept. 19, 1881.

[1] St. John's Gospel, xi. 50.

## GARFIELD'S RIDE AT CHICKAMAUGA.

### [SEPTEMBER 20, 1863.]

#### BY HEZEKIAH BUTTERWORTH.

AGAIN the summer-fevered skies
   The breath of autumn calms;
Again the golden moons arise
   On harvest-happy farms.
The locusts pipe, the crickets sing
   Among the falling leaves,
And wandering breezes sigh, and bring
   The harp-notes of the sheaves.

Peace smiles upon the hills and dells;
   Peace smiles upon the seas;
And drop the notes of happy bells
   Upon the fruited trees.
The broad Missouri stretches far
   Her commerce-gathering arms,
And multiply on Arkansaw
   The grain-encumbered farms.

Old Chattanooga, crowned with green,
   Sleeps 'neath her walls in peace;
The Argo has returned again,
   And brings the Golden Fleece.
O nation! free from sea to sea,
   In union blessed forever,
Fair be their fame who fought for thee
   By Chickamauga River.

The autumn winds were piping low,
   Beneath the vine-clad eaves;
We heard the hollow bugle blow
   Among the ripened sheaves.
And fast the mustering squadrons passed
   Through mountain portals wide,
And swift the blue brigades were massed
   By Chickamauga's tide.

It was the sabbath; and in awe
   We heard the dark hills shake,
And o'er the mountain turrets saw
   The smoke of battle break.

And 'neath that war-cloud, gray and grand,
   The hills o'erhanging low,
The Army of the Cumberland,
   Unequal, met the foe!

Again, O fair September night!
   Beneath the moon and stars,
I see, through memories dark and bright,
   The altar-fires of Mars.
The morning breaks with screaming guns
   From batteries dark and dire,
And where the Chickamauga runs
   Red runs the muskets' fire.

I see bold Longstreet's darkening host
   Sweep through our lines of flame,
And hear again, "The right is lost!"
   Swart Rosecrans exclaim.
"But not the left," young Garfield cries:
   "From that we must not sever,
While Thomas holds the field that lies
   On Chickamauga River!"

Oh! on that day of clouded gold,
   How, half of hope bereft,
The cannoneers, like Titans, rolled
   Their thunders on the left!
I see the battle-clouds again,
   With glowing autumn splendors blending:
It seemed as if the gods with men
   Were on Olympian heights contending.

Through tongues of flame, through meadows brown,
   Dry valley roads concealed,
Ohio's hero dashes down
   Upon the rebel field.
And swift, on reeling charger borne,
   He threads the wooded plain,
By twice a hundred cannon mown,
   And reddened with the slain.

But past the swathes of carnage dire,
   The Union guns he hears,
And gains the left, begirt with fire,
   And thus the heroes cheers—

"While stands the left, yon flag o'erhead,
　　Shall Chattanooga stand!"
"Let the Napoleons rain their lead!"
　　Was Thomas's command.

Back swept the gray brigades of Bragg;
　　The air with victory rung;
And Wurzel's "Rally round the flag!"
　　'Mid Union cheers was sung.
The flag on Chattanooga's height
　　In twilight's crimson waved,
And all the clustered stars of white
　　Were to the Union saved.

O chief of staff! the nation's fate
　　That red field crossed with thee,
The triumph of the camp and state,
　　The hope of liberty!
O nation! free from sea to sea,
　　With union blessed forever,
Not vainly heroes fought for thee
　　By Chickamauga River.

In dreams I stand beside the tide
　　Where those old heroes fell:
Above the valleys long and wide
　　Sweet rings the sabbath bell.
I hear no more the bugle blow,
　　As on that fateful day:
I hear the ringdove fluting low,
　　Where shaded waters stray.

On Mission Ridge the sunlight streams
　　Above the fields of fall,
And Chattanooga calmly dreams
　　Beneath her mountain-wall.
Old Lookout Mountain towers on high,
　　As in heroic days,
When 'neath the battle in the sky
　　Were seen its summits blaze.

'Twas ours to lay no garlands fair
　　Upon the graves "unknown:"
Kind Nature sets her gentians there,
　　And fall the sear leaves lone.

Those heroes' graves no shaft of Mars
  May mark with beauty ever;
But floats the flag of forty stars
  By Chickamauga River.

---

## THE MINUTE-BELLS.

### BY T. H. C.

[From The Transcript.]

There passed a sound, at midnight, through the land,
  A solemn sound of sorrow and of fear, —
  A sound that fell on every wakening ear
Bearing a message all could understand, —
The good, brave chief struck by the assassin's hand,
  The choice of *one*, but to *all* parties dear;
  A patriot, honest, upright, and sincere,
In presence noble, and in action grand.
  And now that death, through weeks of agony,
    Has led him to his rest, the nation sends,
    Like Egypt in her tenth and final blow,
Through all the land a loud and bitter cry;
    And feels, like her, as o'er her dead she bends,
    There is in every home a present woe.

---

## PRESIDENT GARFIELD.

[From The London Spectator.]

The hush of the sick-room; the muffled tread;
  Fond, questioning eye; mute lip, and listening ear;
  Where wife and children watch, 'twixt hope and fear,
A father's, husband's living-dying bed! —
The hush of a great nation, when its head
  Lies stricken! Lo! along the streets he's borne,
  Pale, through rank'd crowds, this gray September morn,
'Mid straining eyes, sad brows unbonneted,
And reverent speechlessness! — a "people's voice!"
  Nay, but a people's silence! through the soul
  Of the wide world its subtler echoes roll,
O brother nation! England for her part
  Is with thee: God willing, she whose heart
Throbbed with thy pain shall with thy joy rejoice.

Sept. 6, 1881.

## JAMES A. GARFIELD.

[From Andrews's American Queen.]

Speak softly; for the midnight bell has tolled,
 And o'er the living world the news has sped
 That he who gave his life for us is dead,
Our loved one that was cast in knightly mould.

Tread gently till that treasured form is laid
 Beneath the sod he would have died to save.
 He who on earth was bravest of the brave
Now sleeps in peace, none making him afraid.

Weep sorely; for our hearts are sore to-day
 For him who calmly suffered and was strong, —
 For him who bore a cruel, bitter wrong,
That centuries of tears can never wash away.

Speak kindly: let us chant our hero's praise,
 And sing of deeds that won him deathless fame;
 So that our children may revere his name,
And learn the mighty truths of former days.

Tell proudly how, with penury's chill hand,
 This son of freedom fought his way to place;
 Passing his compeers in the upward race,
Until he stood the foremost in the land.

Tread softly: he is gone, the good, the just,
 Our noble Garfield, loved above his peers.
 Be ours the pride within the coming years
To cherish those he loved, — the people's trust.

---

## IN MEMORIAM.

### BY MRS. EVA M<sup>c</sup>NAIR PARSONS.

[From Louisville Courier-Journal.]

There cometh a moan on the autumn air:
'Tis the wail of a nation's dark despair;
And its echoes athwart the billows sweep
Of the mighty ocean, dark and deep.
In accents low says the voice of dread, —
"Our chieftain is numbered with the dead."

Crushed by the murderer's fatal shot,
Now low he lies: while a loathsome blot
Made by the deed our banner bears;
And the constant rain of a nation's tears,
And the law's reward, and the hangman's due,
And the curse of the noble, brave, and true,
Can ne'er to its spotless woof restore
The pure and pristine hues it wore.

Nothing can waken and stir again
The busy thoughts of that silent brain;
Nought of the chemist's or surgeon's skill
Bring to the pulses the life's glad thrill:
Worn with its struggle, the body's guest,
The tireless spirit, has soared to rest.

O Goddess of Liberty, veil thy face!
Plant thou a cypress within the place
Where once in its glory and grandeur grew
The chartered worth of our freedom new,
And, over our blood-bought victories past,
The dreary pall of bereavement cast.

O patriots, rise and avenge the deed!
No longer the brazen Moloch feed,
Which stretches its arms both far and wide,
For the gains of dishonor, fraud, and pride;
Defiles the waters which flood the state
With poisoned draughts of revenge and hate;
While virtue in widowed sorrow weeps
Above the couch where her victim sleeps.

LOUISVILLE, KY., Sept. 20, 1881.

## THE SOBBING OF THE BELLS.

(*MIDNIGHT, SEPTEMBER 19-20.*)

### BY WALT WHITMAN.

THE sobbing of the bells, the sudden death-news everywhere,
The slumberers rouse, the rapport of the People,
(Full well they know that message in the darkness,
Full well return the sad reverberations,)
The passionate toll and clang—city to city, joining, sounding, passing,
Those heart-beats of a Nation in the night.

[*From a forthcoming volume.*]

## GARFIELD.

[From Puck.]

Lay him to sleep whom we have learned to love;
    Lay him to sleep whom we have learned to trust.
    No blossom of hope shall spring from out his dust;
No flower of faith shall bloom his sod above.

Although the sod by sorrowful hands be drest,
    Although the dust with tenderest tears be drenched,
    A feebler light succeeds the new light quenched,
And weaker hands the strong hands crossed in rest.

Our new, our untried leader — when he rose,
    Though still old hatreds fed upon old griefs,
    Death or disgrace had stilled the cry of chiefs
Of old who rallied us against our foes.

A soldier of the camp, we knew him thus:
    No saintly champion, high above his kind,
    To follow with devotion mad and blind, —
He fought and fared, essayed and erred, with us.

And so, half-hearted, went we where he led;
    And, following whither beckoned his bright blade,
    Learned his high will and purpose undismayed;
And brought him all our faith — and found him dead.

Is of the sacred pall, that once of yore
    Draped Lincoln dead, one mouldering fragment left?
    Spread it above him, — knight whose helm was cleft
Fair in the fight, as his who fell before.

As his who fell before, his seat we dress
    With pitiful shreds of black, that flow and fail
    Upon the bosom of the breeze, whose wail
Prays us respect that hallowed emptiness.

Ay! who less worthy now may take that chair,
    If our first martyr's spirit on one hand
    And this new ghost upon the other stand,
Saying, Betray thy country if thou dare!

## GARFIELD.

### BY JAMES FRANKLIN FITTS.

[From The Philadelphia North-American.]

#### *CHICKAMAUGA, SEPT. 19, 1863.*

UNDAUNTED 'mid the whirlwind storm of war,
  The shock of surging foes, the wild dismay
  Of shattered legions, swept in blood away,
While the red conflict, thundering afar,
  Raged on the left — yet all unseen, unknown —
  Great chieftain! man of men! 'twas thine alone,
With faith and courage high, the guiding star
  Of that disastrous field, to seek the fray
  Where still the hosts of Union hold their own,
With wasting lines that stand, and strive, and bleed,
  Waiting the promise of a better day.
O steadfast soul! O heart of oak! No harm
Could reach thee then: thou hadst for shield His arm
Who kept thee for the nation's later need.

#### *ELBERON, SEPT. 19, 1881.*

Gone are the weary, woeful weeks of pain;
  Dead are a nation's hopes, and hot her tears.
  The immemorial cycle of the years
Of people's woe completes itself again.
And thou, great soul! — that through these times of peace
  Hast with thy highest might that nation served,
  And best endeavor; who hast never swerved
From right, midst faction's brawl that will not cease,
And who, through all these carking months of woe,
  Hast held thyself as patient and serene
  As when on Chickamauga's field between
The eddying lines that wavered to and fro
  Like stormy ocean tides, thou didst demean
  Thyself the hero, — enter now thy rest!
    A nation's grief shall keep thy memory green,
    A nation's love enshrine thee in her breast.

LOCKPORT, N.Y.

## HE LOVED OUR CRAFT.

### BY E. S. B.

[From The Publishers' Weekly.]

Not as for one who held with steady hand
The centred interests of his native land,
Not for a leader lost, a patriot dead,
Alone our grief is spent, our tears are shed:
We mourn a mind at rest, a great brain stilled,
A noble intellect in madness killed.
He loved our craft of books, that gives to man
The garnered thoughts that past and present span,
A tireless student still he reads the page
That yields life-lessons both from wit and sage.
So, while we mourn our stricken ruler slain,
Our deeper loss but gives us deeper pain.

---

## GARFIELD.

### BY ARTHUR N. WILLCUTT.

[From The Boston Post.]

The lightning rends the mighty oak,
    And hurls it prostrate to the earth:
The power that gave the deadly stroke
    Returns to whence it had its birth.

But nevermore will come again
    To life the oak, or life to man:
Its glory was its earthly bane,
    The height to which its measure ran.

So Garfield fell! the assassin's hand
    Was but the force that moves unseen,
A test, perhaps, for our loved land
    To try its faith, — on God to lean.

Maybe some duty unfulfilled,
    Some wrongful act to race or creed,
Has made the nation's life thus spilled
    A sacrifice to atone the deed.

And while a wail goes o'er the land
    At Garfield's brutal, bloody fall.
Let North and South united stand,
    And trust in Him who ruleth all.

## A NATION'S SORROW.

### BY JOHN READE.

[From The Montreal Gazette.]

"Is this the end of our waiting and hoping so long?
   O Death, thou hast taken our hero! The vigorous will
Is powerless now; and the heart, so tender and strong,
   So patient and loving to all, at last is still.

"Oh! that such as he should be stricken down in his prime,
   By a craven hand, out of fifty millions and more!
We shall know what it means, no doubt, in God's good time;
   But now we question in vain, and our hearts are sore.

"Thou hast pierced with thy sting, O Death! a nation's heart:
   Could nought but our noblest and wisest have sufficed?
We would bow to His will, whose servant, O Death! thou art;
   But oh! must Barabbas be ever preferred to Christ?

"O God! thou knowest, whatever our sins have been,
   That he whom we mourn to-day was loyal and good:
His aims were honest, his heart and his hands were clean,
   He never followed in evil the multitude.

"True patriot ever, true martyr,—what nobler life
   Lives in the world's great record of deathless fame?
And ages hence, when hushed are these sounds of strife,
   A grander nation in honor will hold his name.

"Even now, as we stand by our soldier-statesman's grave,
   The martyr-seed gives promise of blessed fruit:
Baffled and wan, Sedition forgets to rave,
   And Faction, ashamed, has been stricken stark and mute.

"From former foes comes a voice of generous sorrow,
   And North and South have united their tears for the slain;
While afar through the mist of our grief shines the dawn of a morrow
   When to conflict peace shall succeed, and gladness to pain."

   . . . . . . . . . .

Such is the wail that we hear on the southern breeze,
   From a kindred race for a ruler of noble heart;
Not unknown to us, too, are such awful sorrows as these,
   And fain, if we could, would we neighborly solace impart.

O wife and children dear! O mother revered!
  While your nation weeps with you for its martyred chief,
His memory makes you to all mankind endeared,
  And monarch and peasant share alike in your grief.

God grant you comfort, bereaved ones, and pitying love,
  To whom the widow and orphan are ever dear,
And bring you at last to that happy home above,
  Where friends part never, and love casts out all fear.

. . . . . . . .

Thy ways, O God! are far as east to west from ours;
  Thou seest of all that happens beginning, middle, and end;
What now is bitter seed may one day be sweet flowers,
  And what seems now so dark to light and joy may tend.

Even in this sad season of a nation's fiery trial,
  And searching of the hearts of men that sit on high,
'Tis well to know, that, in an age of doubting and denial,
  There are such men as Garfield was, in faith to live and die.

---

## IN MEMORIAM.

### BY LILIAN WHITING.

[From The Cincinnati Commercial.]

OH! where shall we lay our deep sorrow?
  How speak of our loss?
Since our hero, our martyr, is given
  The crown for the cross?

Since he, our ruler, our leader,
  Our nation's true guide,
Has entered that rest which remaineth
  In the fair summer-tide?

He has fought the good fight; he has entered
  The rest that God gave;
And the lives he has blessed bring the tribute
  We lay on his grave.

For all, in his presence benignant,
  Were exalted and cheered;
And virtue seemed more to be cherished,
  And sin to be feared.

Our country, whose lessons our martyr
  So faithfully taught,
Brings its tears and its love, — ay, its gladness,
  For the work that he wrought.

Bring your gratitude, country immortal,
  O'er land and o'er sea!
For the tears of two nations shall mingle,
  Our hero, for thee!

Oh! still from that life thou has entered,
  Behold us, we pray;
Vouchsafe still to guide and direct us,
  And teach us the way.

And so, in the hush of the autumn,
  In its silence and calm,
We will gather the few leaves of healing,
  For sorrow a balm;

And remember his greatness, his honor,
  His rare culture and grace,
His rich gifts and firm faith that no other
  Can hope to replace.

And still will the God of the nations
  Make our sorrow a shrine
When we wait, in sublime aspirations,
  The guidance divine!

BOSTON, Sept. 21, 1881.

---

## OUR DEAD PRESIDENT.

### BY C. H. C.

[From The New-York Tribune.]

WHO has the fitting word,
When every breast is stirred
  With sorrow far too deep for words to tell?
Yet as, amid death's gloom,
Friends whisper in the room,
  We speak of him who lived and died so well.

Night reigned beside the sea,
When morning came to thee,
  Long-waiting heart, so patient and so brave!
Light fell upon thy door,
Pain ceased forevermore,
  Back to its Maker fled the life he gave.

  Like messengers in quest,
  Then started east and west
   Two tidal waves of sorrow round the world:
  Millions of eyes were wet
  Before the tidings met
   Where in the Eastern seas our flags are furled.

  Quickly, through throbbing wire,
  Those waves of sorrow dire
   Awoke across the land the mournful bells:
  Men roused, and could not sleep;
  For, pulsing strong and deep,
   All hearts that knew were ringing funeral knells.

  Wives gazed in husbands' eyes,
  And tears would slowly rise
   For her who fought with Death so long alone;
  And children with no task
  Were left themselves to ask,
   Why Death this father took, and not their own.

  On all the shadow falls:
  It hushes college halls,
   It consecrates the cabins of the West;
  The freedmen loved him well;
  Soldiers his praises tell;
   The rudest boatman is too sad to jest.

  Still, over hills and dells,
  The beautiful sad bells
   Repeat the nation's sorrow for her son;
  But he doth hear the chime
  Of a more peaceful clime
   Than Mentor's fields or quiet Elberon.

  Like him, the Crucified,
  He, who so calmly died,
   Has made the world the better for his pain:
  Surely we now may know
  Our leader was laid low
   To lift the nation to a higher plane.

  We say as once he said, —
  Our hero-ruler dead, —
   "The Lord still reigns, the country is secure."
  There's none can fill his place:
  Rule Thou, O God of grace!
   And guide us on to days more bright and pure.

## LAKE-VIEW CEMETERY.

#### BY W. D. KELLY.

[From The Boston Pilot.]

God rest his soul! and may the victor's crown
   Of immortality inwreathe his head
   Whose spirit from its mortal frame has fled!
Sadly and reverently we lay him down,
While, tolling in the city and the town,
   The bells ring requiems for our ruler dead;
   But all the tears that sympathy can shed
Serve not the sorrow of our hearts to drown,
Who recognize that he, whose noble life
   Such woeful termination murder wrought,
Was sacrificed in an ignoble strife,
   Where worthless demagogues for office fought,
Where greed was uppermost, and passion rife,
   And honesty of purpose valued nought.

Back from the seaside, where but yesterday
   We bore him in the hope the breezy shore
   His failing forces might again restore,
Only to see them slowly waste away;
Into the Capitol, where, while he lay,
   The spirits of the great men gone before,
   His predecessors in its halls of yore,
Kept watch and guard above his pulseless clay;
To this fair city of the mighty West,
   To the broad bosom of his native State,
That nursed him for us on her hardy breast,
   And sent him forth to this untoward fate,
We bring his soulless shape, that it may rest
   Within his mother's keeping and estate.

But he is hers no more! the people claim
   Him as their heritage; and on the scrolls
   Where Immortality the names enrolls
Of those whose lives have won undying fame,
Their hands have written Garfield's, and the same
   Shall have a charm to move our children's souls
   As long as democratic pride controls
Their hearts, and murder be accounted shame:

The South shall vie in praises with the North,
   The East yield not in worship to the West,
But all alike pay homage to his worth,
   Who, if he failed in some things, stood the test
Of his last, greatest trial, and went forth
     Out of his own land, mourned by all the rest.

No king was he! but never king, I trow,
   Wore richer diadems than these our love
   Places to-day his poor, pale brows above.
We could not crown him while he lived; but now
That he has gone from us, our hands endow
   Him with the sceptre, and our hearts approve
   Whatever honors patriotism may move
The land to give him: fifty millions bow
In grief beside this Presidential grave,
   Where the dark cypresses their branches toss,
Who mourn that neither prayer nor skill could save
   Their country from the anguish of his loss,
And each one feels the crowns that monarchs have,
   Compared to his, are vile and worthless dross.

And thus we leave him in his narrow bed,
   Anear the margin of yon placid lake,
   Where the soft music of the waves that break
Upon the sandy shores beneath us spread,
Sing their eternal requiems for the dead;
   But what can heal the wounds that bleed and ache
   In hearts that loved him for his own dear sake,
And will not in their grief be comforted!
O Christ! who, when the widow lost her son,
   Gave him back life to ease his mother's dole ;
With whom the endless ages are but one,
   That has no origin, that knows no goal,—
We do not murmur that thy will is done,
   But crave thy rest for this beloved soul.

AN ELEGANT EDITION

OF

# THE POETS' TRIBUTES

TO

# GARFIELD,

In cloth and gilt binding, is now in preparation.

---

IT WILL CONTAIN MANY ADDITIONAL POEMS.

---

Postpaid, $1.00 a copy. Sold by every bookseller in the United States.

---

MOSES KING . . PUBLISHER,

CAMBRIDGE.

www.ingramcontent.com/pod-product-compliance
Lightning Source LLC
Chambersburg PA
CBHW031607110426
42742CB00037B/1315